The Elements of Legal Prose

The Elements of Legal Prose

Norma Procopiow
University of Maryland

Allyn and Bacon
Boston London Toronto Sydney Tokyo Singapore

Vice President: *Eben W. Ludlow*
Editorial Assistant: *Tania Sanchez*
Senior Marketing Manager: *Lisa Kimball*
Editorial-Production Administrator: *Donna Simons*
Editorial-Production Service: *Susan Freese, Communicáto, Ltd.*
Text Design/Electronic Composition: *Denise Hoffman*
Composition Buyer: *Linda Cox*
Manufacturing Buyer: *Suzanne Lareau*
Cover Administrator: *Jenny Hart*

A Viacom Company
160 Gould Street
Needham Heights, MA 02494

Internet: www.abacon.com

Between the time website information is gathered and then published, it is not unusual for some sites to have closed. Also, the transcription of URLs can result in unintended typographical errors. The publisher would appreciate notification where these occur so that they may be corrected in subsequent editions.

Library of Congress Cataloging-in-Publication Data

Procopiow, Norma.
The elements of legal prose / Norma Procopiow.
p. cm. — (The elements of composition series)
Includes bibliographical references and index.
ISBN 0-205-28225-3 (alk. paper)
1. Legal composition. I. Title. II. Series.
KF250.P76 1999
808'.06634—dc21 98-48345
CIP

Printed in the United States of America

10 9 8 7 6 5 4 3 2 1 03 02 01 00 99 98

For Andrea, Julie, and Stefanie

Contents

To the Instructor

The Elements of Legal Prose is about the study of writing legal prose, a form of writing with unique rhetorical strategies. This book offers a brief guide to the skills that will facilitate students' practical writing tasks. Since it is apparent that generic writing classes no longer serve those whose vocations involve discourses governed by legal logic, this text addresses the specific writing needs of clearly articulating the basic components and formats found in good legal prose. Its six chapters present the special ways of thinking and writing about a subject in which anything incomplete or inexact could have serious consequences.

Features of this text include the following:

- It can serve as a primary or secondary textbook for a number of law-related courses and subject areas, such as paralegal programs, government and political science, corrections and criminal justice studies, sociology and the law, psychology and the law, literature and the law, journalism, and undergraduate prelaw writing courses.
- Each chapter provides learning objectives along with accompanying examples to demonstrate those objectives.
- Steps in the process of writing legal prose are discussed, from knowing the audience to preparing the complete argument.
- Examples from student papers illustrate and instruct at a peer level rather than at a more intimidating professional level.
- Each chapter suggests class exercises and writing assignments—some designed for students to prepare in groups, others to prepare individually.
- Model student papers are presented in Appendix B. These papers represent the dominant writing formats analyzed in the text.

This book is intended for instruction in *writing*, not in those various and complex issues of the legal system that are taught in law school.

However, as a textbook on writing legal prose, it incorporates examples and exercises involving both real and imaginary legal issues. These examples and exercises emphasize a kind of legal logic and rhetoric, but they make no pretense to being a casebook for the actual presentation of a legal procedure.

Acknowledgments

My special thanks go to my editor, Eben Ludlow, for his unfailing support and interest throughout this project. I am also indebted to my daughter, Julie Procopiow Todd, Administrative Judge, for her guidance and insight regarding legal technicalities. Finally, I would like to acknowledge Joan Meyler, John Jay College of Criminal Justice, who reviewed this manuscript for Allyn and Bacon and provided useful suggestions.

To the Student

This book is about writing legal prose, a special mode of communication that you will use in a variety of forms and fields. Thus, whether you are preparing to take the Law School Admission Test (LSAT), planning to work in the criminal justice system or a government agency or institution, or studying to be a paralegal, you will need the skills outlined in these chapters.

What, you might ask, distinguishes legal prose from other types of written communication? *Legal prose* exists primarily as that body of rules and policies, decisions and statutes, and reports and case files that define and protect us as a society. The very practical nature of these texts requires that legal prose be objective, clear, and precise. Moreover, legal prose should not unnecessarily limit freedom of expression yet should recognize the rights of others: a challenging order. Finally, legal prose is a special genre whose lifeblood is its language, whether embodied in a Supreme Court opinion, a legislative bill or referendum, a court official's memorandum, or a police officer's report. Whatever its level of writing or its intended audience, its objectives, basic organizational strategies, and rhetorical techniques remain constant.

Good legal prose often matches the eloquence of literary classics. Indeed, certain legal texts are quoted not only for their decisive, significant content but also for the style that enhances that content. This is partly because the essence of law is a highly metaphoric, or figurative, phenomenon. For example, the structure of the trial in the U.S. court system is a legal metaphor. That is, it carries a basic symbolic meaning beyond the standard concepts of negotiation, advocacy, and rules we routinely identify as the "nuts and bolts" of the law. The elements of this symbolic system may be seen in Blind Justice, the figure whose eyes are covered, holding the scales—a metaphor for the power that weighs and resolves conflicting claims. This figure primarily represents the notion that all parties are equal when seeking justice. This may be seen by trial participants as a dynamic process: the judge as the centerpiece that holds and controls the pans for the scales, ensuring that no false weights are thrown in; the jury watching the scales to determine which of the scales is lower; and the defense and prosecution providing the weights that tip or balance the scales. It is inspiring to envision the law in this way as well as in a practical way. It elevates our concept of legal prose as the workmanship of a special, honored craft.

Following is a brief description of the content of each chapter in this text. Together, these chapters form the stepping stones that will help you write legal prose with confidence and skill.

Plan of the Book

Chapter 1: Writing to an Audience

Legal situations and those individuals or legal constituencies immediately affected by such situations differ in a variety of ways. Consequently, you sometimes will be required to produce a document in very formal language. At other times, you will have to envelop an argument in subtle innuendo rather than in direct adversarial prose. In yet other circumstances, it will be advisable to write in a style commonly referred to as *plain English.*

It is necessary to start with a clear understanding of your audience before concentrating on rhetorical tactics. For example, suppose that you are an intern for an association that lobbies for state regulation of physician-assisted suicide and you are asked to draft a position paper for a senior citizen organization. You urge the organization to propose an initiative on this issue, which will be submitted to a state legislator. How would your argument, as directed to the senior citizen group, differ from one that makes the same appeal to a Christian coalition organization—a potentially more resistant audience? In each instance, your level of information and tone will need to be adjusted to consider their opposing needs and values.

Chapter 2: Legal Definition

Whenever you wish to sound and *be* authoritative, your credibility depends on providing substantial definitions of the key words and phrases in your document. Some standard terms will remain unchanged whether you depend on an ordinary dictionary, a law dictionary, or another form of reference such as an encyclopedia. On the other hand, certain terms will be defined or qualified differently according to a particular jurisdiction or state. You may also find that certain terms will acquire new or supplemental meanings over time. This generally comes about when case facts bring in new, unprecedented actions or conditions.

Legal definitions often have several layers or contexts; words and phrases are defined in an intentionally broad fashion to allow for flexibility and discretion in decisions. For example, does the term *flag desecration* refer equally to burning a flag during a political demonstration and wearing a flag patch on the backside of jeans in a parade? To some degree, the conclusion reached will depend on several factors: the political climate in which the term *desecration* is interpreted, the individual leanings or biases of the judiciary members, and the specific circumstances of the alleged desecration.

Chapter 3: Style in Legal Prose

Style in legal prose shares many features with the styles of other forms of prose. At the same time, it is an exacting medium of communication using criteria specifically governed by the existing body of law.

By and large, style in legal prose will assume different forms, depending on who will be influenced by the content embedded in the texts involved. The following are the four main categories of individuals or groups that are influenced by or produce legal prose:

- The citizens who are affected by the statutes, regulations, court decisions, and rules
- The attorneys and other representatives of the legal system who act on behalf of these people
- The members of the judiciary, who write decisions and case law
- The legislators, who enact the laws

Although it is unlikely that you will draft a document to a Supreme Court Justice (but this may become a reality in the future), there are a number of instances in which you will write to a lawmaker, an attorney, a group, or a particular individual. Your style will undoubtedly be different in each of these instances, but you should consider the following:

- The pragmatic implications of *how* you write
- The need for clarity of statement in your writing
- The forcefulness of your statement, argument, or appeal
- The word choice, or diction
- The effectiveness of citing relevant constitutional provisions, rules, case law, statutes, and so on

Chapter 4: Narrative in Legal Prose

Narrative pervades every aspect of legal prose. Whether you are writing a family will, a police officer's report, a vehicular injury claim, or a victim impact statement, some element of story will appear in your material. This seems most apparent when you study the details of a criminal trial, since the patterns of motives or evidence disclosed in a trial often resemble fiction. But narrative exists in less sensational forms of legal prose, as well.

Although narrative has always played an important role in legal transactions, it has become even more important today. There is increasing demand for the use of story in the law. This movement toward a narrative approach has been seen as especially empowering for minorities and other marginal groups, who claim that "legalese" in language perpetuates the elitist power structure that governs us. According to these groups, stories *particularize* individuals, whereas "legalese" renders them as abstract entities, having little humanity.

In addition to this call for greater use of narrative by these groups, we have become a media-obsessed society that follows legal issues presented in the forms of news coverage as well as entertainment coverage. Thus, the media have brought a greater fusion of politics and public values to the law. The use of narrative has become an effective linchpin for these intersecting spheres.

Chapter 5: Writing the Argument

Argument in rhetoric has traditionally fallen under the general rubric of persuasion. Persuasion may take various forms in writing, such as a letter calculated to flatter someone or a convincing description of goals on a subject. Consequently, persuasion is loosely associated with the ability to arouse emotion. In addition, argument is that form of persuasion intended to establish the truth or falsity of a proposition or—to use more legalistic terminology—the truth or falsity of a charge, claim, or allegation. Although persuasion is more often associated with an aptness of language that leads people to believe what is written, the terms *persuasion* and *argument* are often used interchangeably.

In this text, I use *argument* to mean that part of legal prose that directly presents the pros and cons of an issue. There are four important steps to keep in mind when preparing an argument:

1. Select the facts and collect the evidence with care.
2. Apply the appropriate legal theories and rules.
3. Bring a logical order and management to your position and to its accompanying refutations.
4. Provide a conclusion that fully connects the facts and evidence with the laws that support those facts and evidence.

For example, how would you organize a position paper in a jurisdiction where casino gambling is illegal and the fire fighters' organization argues that revenue from such gaming would make possible the purchase of needed fire trucks? There would undoubtedly be a range of conflicting reactions by interested parties here, from those who endorse this proposal as a benefit to the community; to those who feel gambling depletes family finances, which eventually costs the state more in assistance programs; and to those who condemn gambling as a threat to society's moral fiber. Such an issue requires careful coverage of the following in the four steps (just enumerated) of your argument:

1. The claims being made on all sides regarding the issue
2. Recent law (e.g., statutory and case law) and jurisdictional trends regarding the legalization of casino gambling
3. Evidence from jurisdictions where casino gambling *is* legal and has brought revenue for community services
4. A conclusion that coordinates the reasons for such an appeal with the applicable legal rulings

Chapter 6: Research in Legal Writing

Your writing must be *reliable* in order to be effective. It is necessary to learn how to gather information in the library as well as electronically in order to utilize authoritative research materials and deploy them to your best advantage. As you inquire into an actual problem or issue, you can quickly access the original data you will need by using an explicit research methodology. The manner in which you present research—the delivery technique—will weigh heavily in the success of your argument.

The treatment of legal research in this text follows a fundamental approach, not intended for law students and lawyers, and will include the following:

- Where and how to look for primary and secondary sources
- The hierarchy of legal types
- The distinction among the three types of legal authority
- When and how to cite legal documents
- The step-by-step search process in a law library

Appendix A: Advancing in the Field: The Application Process

Appendix A addresses the practical issue of how to apply to law school or to some law-related professional, educational, or internship program. It is intended to provide you with direction regarding the different steps in an application process. Guidelines are offered on how to prepare for the entire admissions procedure. The following are the most common components, or steps, in this process: an essay, a letter of application, a resumé, and an interview. Instructions as well as models are provided for each of these steps.

Appendix B: Sample Papers

Appendix B provides four student samples that serve as models of the dominant writing formats analyzed in this text. These samples are accompanied by evaluative comments, indicating where and how the student applies the most effective writing strategy for the intended purpose.

Glossary of Legal Terms

A number of legal terms appear in this book, especially in the writing examples that cite or refer to court decisions. To provide a better understanding of these examples, this text contains a glossary of brief, simple definitions of those technical terms that have different meanings in the law than in lay discourse.

The Elements of Legal Prose

1

Writing to an Audience

Why Write Legal Prose?

This chapter begins with a simple question: Why write legal prose? Here are some fundamental reasons:

- To organize information and present reasoning, in order to reach agreement on the rules and laws that govern our day-to-day business transactions and personal relations
- To clarify those actions and forms of behavior that are allowable and those that are prohibited, under the legal codes of our country
- To prepare both advisory and argumentative documents in connection with a case

Range of Subject Areas

Given these reasons, the range of subject areas in legal prose is vast; the range of importance attributed to each area is equally vast. Indeed, most of our official transactions are governed by and inscribed in some type of legalistic document. A common transaction will serve as a good example. When you rent a house or purchase a car, a contract or warranty is needed to specify the terms agreed upon by the participating parties. As a (hopefully) less common example, that same house or car may become the subject of some kind of legal action, as a result of theft, defects in performance, or a similar reason. Here, the documents would be more numerous and more complex.

Thus, you are learning an important craft, one that serves both the law and the circumstances of a particular audience. As writers of legal prose, rather than functioning as mere processors of texts, you are, in a sense, problem solvers, playing an active and often exciting role in the legal world. How do you begin? Consider your audience.

Kinds of Audiences

"Just do it."

"You deserve a break today, at McDonald's."

Imagine the time and cost invested by huge corporations such as Nike and McDonald's to create commercials—all in search of the right message to sell their products. The first step in this search is to identify the particular audience the corporation wants to reach. Consequently, "Just do it" has been aimed at the sports-minded, youthful in spirit consumer. The slogan has a tone that appeals to this particular audience's sense of adventure; at the same time, it subtly urges the consumers to purchase the corporation's sports equipment. The McDonald's jingle also targets an audience: those earnest, hard-working people—namely *you*—who deserve to relax for a while, especially at a McDonald's restaurant.

When writing legal prose, as in advertising, it is important to know your readers—or audience. Audiences are bound to differ in their levels of legal expertise, education, attitude, and needs. Thus, when preparing legal documents, the first challenge is to learn as much as possible about the targeted audience. You can then use the most fitting rhetorical tools to present your material. Let us first consider the basic kinds of audience you will find yourself writing to and then discuss how you would organize the most appropriate document for each. We will use examples of legal issues that arise in individual cases, as well as in public forums, and discuss strategies for writing to targeted audiences on each.

You will prepare documents for these kinds of audiences:

- The general public
- The client
- The attorney, the judge, the legislator
- The political or government establishment
- Administrative agencies

Sometimes memberships in these audience groups will overlap and you will need to appeal simultaneously to more than one type; this requires discretion and careful use of language. Two situations immediately suggest themselves:

1. Your audiences are divided, perhaps on the level of their legal training. Here, one *subject* must be presented in language with which several persons or groups will be most comfortable. Examples 1.1, An Abused Spouse, and 1.2, Mandatory School Uniforms, which follow, spell out the various kinds of writing to use in this situation.
2. You must address one *audience* but an audience self-divided, perhaps a legislative or administrative committee, in which the members hold opposing views on the issue you wish to present. Example 1.3, Casino Gambling, provides such a case and offers possible strategies.

Strategies for Various Audiences

As you plan your writing strategies for various audiences, here are some suggestions:

- Conduct background research to determine your audience's direct needs and interests regarding the subject.
- Get information regarding their familiarity with and bias toward the subject.
- Select the kind of argument they will best accept as both reasonable and objective.

EXAMPLE 1.1 An Abused Spouse

Let us suppose that you are the attorney for Mrs. Miller, an abused spouse, who has come to you for legal services. You have had a consultation and must now prepare a letter to her regarding action to be taken to protect herself and to obtain a divorce. You must also send a letter to her husband's attorney, informing him of the basis of Mrs. Miller's action against his client. Your third letter will be to a judge, discussing a technicality that will figure in the case. Each of these letters is a kind of legal communication; each will be written differently to suit your intended audience.

Letter to Client

In this letter, you should be cordial and supportive, explaining in simple terms the practical steps you and your client discussed when you met. In this document, you should not burden Mrs. Miller with formal prose regarding binding issues; that is reserved for the contract you have drawn up. The letter should contain language such as the following:

> It would be helpful if you would collect the following information before our next meeting: a) an accurate list of what accounts are in both your and your husband's names; b) a financial estimate of what you need to subsist on. I have enclosed the standard client/attorney preliminary contract that we discussed at our meeting. If you have any questions regarding its details, feel free to call me.

You need to communicate with Mrs. Miller in a direct way. Be clear and thorough but avoid jargon, citation of precedents, and legal shorthand, which show off your knowledge but are of little help to your client.

Letter to Husband's Attorney

This letter is addressed to someone at your own professional level. However, the attorney is your opponent in this particular case. Therefore, you will need to come to the point quickly, present necessary facts, and find a common meeting ground in which to present your information. The writing should be more formal:

> My client wishes to enter into a contract that will result in a settlement agreeable to both parties, eventuating in a termination of the marriage. Mrs. Miller states that she has suffered repeated abuse by Mr. Miller over the years, and that the abuse has escalated in nature and frequency. She is eligible for spousal privilege and other injunctive actions; the most immediate relief she is entitled to requires that Mr. Miller vacate the residence.

This is a courteous yet firm statement of charges and demands made by Mrs. Miller's attorney. Legal terminology (i.e., declaring "spousal privilege") is kept to a minimum; at the same time, this kind of terminology, rather than a list of accusations, lessens the possibility of emotional counterattack by Mr. Miller's attorney.

Letter to Judge

This letter is also written to a professional audience—the judge presiding in the case. The judge will be impartial, weighing the details of your letter insofar as they relate to jurisdictional laws, rules, and regulations. Therefore, this letter should cite specific codes applicable to your client's grievance. Let us presume that the judge asks you for a preliminary letter—or memorandum—on the "vacate the residence" provision that is being sought. The text should contain language like the following:

> Having determined that the abuse my client, Mrs. Miller, claims she suffers is not just minor "incompatibility fights," but rather a persistent pattern of aggravated spousal assault, I shall request that a Protective Order, as granted by the *Family Law Article §1-203(a),* be imposed. The criteria cited for such injunctive action are applicable to this case and are satisfied in this petition.

This is the most legalistic of the three letters. It has an assertive, though not demanding, tone, offering substantial basis for the request and for a specific legally defined action.

EXAMPLE 1.2 Mandatory School Uniforms

Imagine a situation in a school district where the teachers are experiencing problems with unruly students. The disruption is intensified by a ganglike mood in which the students' personal sense of identity is being gauged by what they wear—perhaps an expensive brand of sneakers or an outfit with insignias that affiliates them with a particular group. In such an atmosphere, delinquency and academic failure have become a problem. To remedy this, school officials propose that uniforms be mandatory. However, this school district includes a fair percentage of low-income families who argue that the uniform policy imposes an additional monetary hardship on them.

With regard to this problem, you might be writing to several kinds of audiences: the parents (to discuss their role); the school board (to discuss a solution); and the American Civil Liberties Union (to discuss a constitutional issue). These audiences obviously differ in legal expertise, education, needs, and attitude. How do you construct the most effective document for each?

To address the parents in what might be considered threatening legalistic prose would more likely alienate them than win them over; an overprecise style can be taken as offensive or intimidating. Yet, clearly, the parents' support is crucial in reaching an agreement. Thus, as an advocate, you will want to deal with all parties in the most appropriate manner—not to deceive but to facilitate exchange. (*Note:* Let us agree to take a position *against* mandatory uniforms.)

Writing to Parents

This audience would probably have little interest in the constitutional debates regarding free speech and dress codes. The parents' immediate concern is the imposition of a financial burden. On the other hand, they are just as concerned about safety in the school environment as the school officials are. They share the school officials' objectives, but they disagree with their remedies. Writing to these parents, therefore, means providing simple information, in clear terms, regarding the pros and cons of mandatory uniforms. Rather than citing landmark Supreme Court decisions on students' constitutional rights, you should discuss safety in schools in a practical way. The following passage suggests the style to use with this audience:

> We realize that while requiring our children to wear uniforms may not be a cure-all, it might possibly alleviate the problem. Our children are coming to school wearing types of clothing that identify them with groups, and, as you must know, these groups are diverse in a number of ways. This creates tension, leading to intimidation and fights. At the same time, the school authorities are being inconsistent: They are unwilling to commit financial resources for uniforms to those in need, yet they provide textbooks without cost to *all* children. Is this fair? We must ask the school board to resolve the dress code in a manner most equitable to everyone in our district.

Writing to School Board

When writing to the school board, you should use a different level of language; you should also satisfy a different need. As a professional entity, the board wants to administer itself efficiently and effectively within the law. Yet it bears the burden of defending its proposal within the limits of arguable infringement of students' constitutional rights of free speech, as expressed in their choice of attire.

It is fair to assume that the school board's chief objective is to improve the quality of education in the district. Hence, when writing your argument to this audience, it would be useful to cite a decision on a former case that offers a workable alternative to mandatory uniforms. The introduction of a legal precedent in such a semiformal context might be handled as follows:

> As the board considers these problems, let us keep in mind a parallel case. In *Pyle v. South Hadley School Committee,*[1] two brothers were enjoined from wearing T-shirts of questionable appropriateness to school. For example, one brother appeared in a shirt that read "See Dick Drink. See Dick Drive. See Dick Die. Don't Be a Dick." The Hadley School Committee argued that "personal appearance should not disrupt the educational process, call singular attention to the individual, violate federal, state, or local health and obscenity laws, or affect the welfare and safety of the students, teachers, or classmates."
>
> The student who wore the shirt was sent home. His father filed suit against the school committee. The U.S. District Court

> relieved the student of punishment. However, in its decision, the court required that the school committee assume a greater responsibility for defining what clothing is offensive and disruptive—that is, the school must provide *specific* guidelines regarding permissible apparel. This ensures standards of decency and decorum without placing undue monetary hardship on poorer families.

Writing to American Civil Liberties Union

The American Civil Liberties Union (ACLU) is an organization noted for the defense of issues relating to First Amendment and other constitutional rights. This involves them in litigation where the interpretation of these rights brings controversy. Consequently, the question of "symbolic expression" and constitutional protection regarding student attire is a matter of importance to the ACLU. A brief review of the problem confronting this school district would enable the ACLU to correlate its *legal* thinking with former decisions on similar issues and indicate the relevance of these precedents to this case. For example, the classic Supreme Court decision on student dress codes is the *Tinker v. Des Moines* ruling.[2] Officials in this Des Moines school district had prohibited students from wearing black armbands to school in protest of the Vietnam War. The students challenged this disciplinary action and the case was brought before the Supreme Court, which decided in the students' favor. When writing to the ACLU, asking them to intercede in your behalf, you could refer to this case as a basis for negotiation:

> We believe that with your support, we may be better able to reach an accord between our school board, which proposes mandatory uniforms, and those parents who view the proposal as favoring only affluent families in our district. As you know, the *Tinker v. Des Moines* decision upheld the students' constitutional rights over the rights of schools to enforce dress codes. We believe this case can be invoked as precedent for upholding our position. This request takes into account the need for judicious management of dress codes by the school board. With the board's cooperation, we may avoid the cost of possible litigation.

EXAMPLE 1.3 Casino Gambling

This example deals with an audience that is homogeneous in its level of sophistication but has mixed views on a proposal. Let us consider an actual issue that has recently prompted controversy in several states—namely, whether to legalize casino gambling. Maryland is one such state confronted with this decision. Suppose you are a lobbyist writing to the Maryland State Legislature, whose members are strongly divided on this proposal. (*Note:* Let us agree to take a position *in favor of* legalizing casino gambling.)

First, here is some factual background pertaining to the sample letter that follows. Two northeastern states—namely, Connecticut and Delaware—have recently legalized casino gambling. Reports indicate that these states have enjoyed a considerable revenue increase from this recreational pastime. Eager to have a "share of the pie," neighboring states are considering legalization in their jurisdictions. For example, the New York State Legislature has started a referendum process that could lead to a ballot on this issue in a future election.

Members of the Maryland Legislature have engaged in heated debate over this issue. How do you prepare a document that both defers to opponents of legalization and supports those who champion your view? A workable strategy is to acknowledge the opposition's reasons while placing them in a larger context that makes them seem less desirable. Thus, you will attempt to show how the benefits of legalizing casino gambling overwhelm the reasons for forbidding it:

Writing to the Legislature

You have deliberated on this proposal with sincerity, bringing forth legitimate arguments and valid statistics. We would like now to consider these points in a somewhat larger context, which we feel in the long run will show that the benefits of legalization weigh heavily toward the welfare of the state.

The crusaders against legalizing casino gambling fear that it will lead to family breakdown and to the loss of productivity and community involvement. But haven't crusaders in the past expressed the same fear about other forms of entertainment? To blame external activities for societal demoralization is to ignore

> individual responsibility. Moreover, for the percentage of those who believe that gambling is a vice, there is an equal percentage of citizens who do not share that view. Our constituents should have the opportunity to decide what is right or wrong for themselves and their families.

Summary of Strategies

The preceding examples are just a sampling of the types of writing to select for various audiences. In certain instances, the task of preparing documents for a resistant or even hostile audience will be difficult. However, if you train yourself to keep in mind the other person's argument, and to acknowledge it without weakening your own argument, the task will be easier. Here are a few tips:

- Determine your points of disagreement.
- Plan a way to acknowledge them.
- Determine your points of agreement.
- Plan a way to build on them.

Reaching Your Audience

Ways to Prepare

Once you have clarified the kind of audience you are writing to, you need to establish the purpose of your document. The most common purposes fall into four categories: to inform, to seek information, to persuade, and to argue. Sometimes these purposes are combined: for example, you may need to provide factual information in order to persuade an audience that one solution is preferable to another.

During this preparatory stage of the process, you must decide *how* to present your document. Here are some ways to accomplish this:

- Choose a voice, or ethos.
- Identify essential information.
- Evaluate the information.

- Formulate a thesis statement.
- Organize an outline.

As you see, organizing an outline is the last step in this list. Once you have analyzed how to proceed with the other items, you are ready to prepare your outline. An outline—if arranged with orderly, logical headings and subdivisions—gives you the skeletal frame on which to develop almost any document. First, let us discuss these steps and then examine some sample outlines.

Choose a Voice, or Ethos

At the beginning of this chapter, I discussed the various types of audience that you will address in legal prose. These types will determine how you must bring *yourself,* the writer, into the picture. How do you do this? You choose a voice, or *ethos* (a Greek term meaning a person's overall disposition or character). A convincing voice makes a good impression; a good impression furthers your purpose. Here are a few rules for creating a convincing voice:

- Keep your voice consistent.
- Choose a voice of reason and integrity.
- Use an authoritative but not patronizing voice.

Your voice in writing legal prose is established through a combination of elements, such as the wording you select and the positioning of those words. The tone you convey is also dependent on word selection. A simple example of word choice involves pronoun usage. If you use *we, us,* and *our* often, these pronouns (known as *communal pronouns*) create a sense of closeness or familiarity with your audience. If you use the pronoun *I* frequently, you might create any of the following types of voice: authoritative and worthy of respect, self-obsessed and indifferent to others, or personal and open. Finally, if you use nouns instead of pronouns in your writing (e.g., *petitioner claimed*) or if you use the pronoun *one* (e.g., *one might argue*), you project yet another voice: formal, impersonal, or legalistic. Generally speaking, choose those pronouns, or any other words, that project to your audience a tone of directness and personal interest.

Look at the difference between these two statements:

Statement A

Appellee petitioned the Clover Lake Planning Commission, regarding a multiple-family residential project, to rezone a five-acre parcel of the land for development of a senior citizen recreation site, inasmuch as there was a substantial representation of elderly purchasers, many of whom are limited in transportation services. Commission denied request and the county officials agreed. Appellee brought suit against county, citing protection under County Court Rule #583, which judicates interests of residents with special needs.

Statement B

John B. Seech, a senior citizen of limited financial means and frail health, petitioned the Clover Lake Planning Commission to rezone a five-acre parcel of the land scheduled for residential development. He emphasized that the project would house many purchasers over age 65. Because of their limitations, both physical and financial, these citizens are not able to travel by automobile to other locations. Moreover, public transportation is infrequent and expensive. Therefore, they need a recreation area within walking distance. When the Commission rejected Mr. Seech's request, he filed suit and claimed that County Court Rule #583 had been created to satisfy just such requests as this.

Statement B is preferable because it conveys the same information as Statement A but in a more simple, humane, and honest voice.

Finally, here is a good rule regarding voice: Ask yourself if *you* would be convinced if someone else were writing to you in this voice. This self-examination places you in a larger framework, making you more objective about your own writing. It also helps you recognize any prejudices that are unconsciously embedded in your writing.

Identify Essential Information

You must plan to place signposts or guidelines early in your document in order to prepare your reader for the material that follows. At first, line up the essential information and group segments of related contents. A correct sequence of the information helps the reader grasp the purpose of the entire document. In order to achieve this, make a list of the large-scale units that you will incorporate. Whatever format your writing assumes, these are the common segment blocks in legal prose:

- Introduction
- Explanation of procedure
- Analysis
- Solution, rationale, or recommendation
- Summary

It is also a good idea to highlight key terms or subjects, so that your reader can identify the facts or questions that will be subsequently analyzed in the document. One way to prepare your audience for what follows is to repeat key or *link* words in your introduction. Although it is tempting to vary your words for stylistic reasons when writing, statements gain coherence from the repetition of link words. The following passage is from an introduction to a report on welfare programs by the U.S. General Accounting Office (GAO) (for emphasis, the link words are italicized):

> Three of the federal government's major welfare *programs* are Aid to Families with Dependent Children (AFDC), Medicaid and Food Stamps. In fiscal year 1990, these *programs* provided over $92 billion in public assistance benefits to about 25 million people. Although the U.S. Department of Health and Human Services (HHS) and U.S. Department of Agriculture (USDA) have overall responsibility for administering the *programs*, states are responsible for determining participants' *eligibility*. To help determine *eligibility* and the amount of assistance people should receive, states rely heavily on computer *systems*. In the last 10 years, the federal government has given states more than $950 million to develop and operate these *systems*.[3]

This paragraph provides a general framework for the three related areas of this report. The repetition of certain words focuses on the points this report will discuss.

Evaluate the Information

When you evaluate the information you are writing about, try to hold in check overly strong opinions. By keeping an objective view, you will avoid sounding argumentative even though you are actually arguing a point. If you are justifying an action, an event, or an issue, take into consideration the results or possible consequences of your position. Anticipate questions or objections that may be posed by your audience; reserve a strategic place in your document for answering them (preferably near the beginning).

You will also want to write a document that is reliable. In order to achieve this, be sure to evaluate the information you have gathered according to these criteria: accuracy, relevance, and importance. Ask yourself the following questions for each:

Accuracy

1. What is the source of your information?
2. Is the person or agency generally trustworthy?
3. Can the information be verified?
4. Are the materials you are using free from ambiguity and self-contradiction?

Relevance

1. Have you gathered materials that are of little direct use to your purpose, even though interesting in themselves?
2. Could your materials, in fact, cloud the issue?

Importance

1. Is the information that you are gathering of such weight that it will be taken seriously by the audience you want to influence?
2. Are there collections of minor details that give an effect of pettiness that may prove detrimental to your position?

Formulate a Thesis Statement

Finally, you can give credence and weight to your writing by selecting those facts that convey vital information and the actuality of circumstances. Once you have collected these facts, you are ready to formulate a thesis; this generally evolves into your purpose statement or the proposition you will prove or analyze. Here is an example of a thesis statement that satisfies the criteria previously discussed:

> Substance abuse in the workplace is a significant national problem. Employers are struggling to find ways to reduce their employees' use of alcohol and drugs. Employers are adopting substance abuse policies which prohibit any illegal use of drugs (including prescription drugs not taken in accordance with a valid prescription) and reporting to work or working under any influence of alcohol. An increasing number of employers have adopted substance abuse testing programs. In deciding whether to institute drug and alcohol testing of applicants and employees, employers should consider the benefits expected to be gained from testing, the cost of testing, the impact of testing on their workforce, and how they will respond to a positive test result.[4]

This statement prepares the reader for an analysis of the numerous legal considerations employers must take into account when deciding whether to institute a testing program for their employees. The statement suggests the necessary components for dealing with this subject. (*Note:* An employer must weigh these components with the privacy rights of the individual.)

Thus, a purpose statement should enumerate and evaluate the leading facts to be analyzed in the document, stimulating the reader to read further. It may or may not suggest the position that will be taken. In this excerpt on drug testing, the writer indicates that the pros and cons of such testing will be given equal validity, leaving the decision to the employers.

Organize an Outline

When you have evaluated the information, you are ready to organize an outline. The time you spend on an outline before you begin writing will save countless hours later on, for these reasons:

1. You can shuffle and reshuffle segments of the outline until you arrive at the best order for your material.
2. You can determine which blocks and units of information belong together.

3. You can create main headings and subheadings and, by doing so, spot omissions or irrelevant information.
4. You can modify areas for the outline according to your ongoing research.
5. You can add new ideas or details to the outline that you had not thought of initially.

Format of Outline. Indentation indicates the importance of your ideas to each other as well as to the main argument. Therefore, you will find yourself constructing a more logical hierarchy of your material through indentation. One way to do this is to label in a descending order from roman numerals to capital letters to arabic numerals to small letters, in this way:

```
I.
    A.
    B.
        1.
        2.
            a.
            b.
```

Sample Outlines. If you structure a good outline, you will have taken an important step toward producing a coherent document. When formatting an outline, keep in mind that headings are your reader's guideposts. They indicate the direction your document is taking; therefore, they must be carefully worded, selected, and positioned. Here are some suggestions for producing a functional yet flexible outline:

- Enumerate the units or blocks of information in accordance with their importance and relevance. If, for example, you are advocating prayer in schools, it is not necessary to include a unit on the faith of the nation's founders.

- Devote a unit of the outline to opposing arguments. There are various ways and places to incorporate opposing arguments. Some rhetoricians believe that it is best to discuss them early on, to reply to or discredit them and get them out of the way. Then, if you continue with *your* position, restating it in your conclusion, the reader has been gently directed toward your view.

• If there is any legal background or case law directly applicable to your subject, include reference to it in your outline.

• Make the subheadings consistent with major units or headings. In effect, subheadings should answer or satisfy the title of the major heading. For example, if your major heading is Current Plea-Bargaining Practices, these might be your subheadings:

A. Charge Agreements
B. Recommendation Agreements
C. Specific Sentence Agreements
D. Fact Stipulation Agreements

• Use parallel headings, which make it easier for readers to find specific sections. In particular, grammatically parallel headings (e.g., sets of noun phrases or sets of verb phrases) prevent the reader from having to sort through different formats.

EXAMPLE 1.4 Physician-Assisted Suicide

The following outline for a position paper advocating physician-assisted suicide contains the recommended components:

I. Summary of Recent Cases
    A. Michigan State
    B. New York State
    C. Washington State
    D. Holland's Case
II. Arguments against Physician-Assisted Suicide
    A. Religious Considerations
    B. "Slippery Slope" Theory
    C. Hospice Care Alternative
III. Constitutionality of Physician-Assisted Suicide
    A. Equal Protection (Fourteenth Amendment)
        1. *Roe v. Wade*
        2. *Planned Parenthood v. Cagey*
        3. Nancy Cruzan
        4. Living Will
    B. First Amendment Separation of Church and State
IV. Recommendations

EXAMPLE 1.5 Casino Gambling

The following outline for a position paper advocating the legalization of casino gambling in Maryland is poorly structured. See if you can detect the flaws in its design:

I. Current Gambling Laws
   A. Maryland
      1. Slot Machines
      2. Casino Nights

II. Models from Other States
   A. Nevada
      1. Benefits
   B. Atlantic City
      1. Benefits
      2. Competition
   C. Louisiana
      1. As a New Entrant
      2. Benefits

III. Analysis of Current Gambling Methods in Maryland
   A. Lotteries
      1. Revenues
   B. Slot Machines
      1. Revenues
   C. Casino Nights
      1. Revenues

IV. Statistical Indicators
   A. Population Base
   B. Per Capita Incomes

V. Maryland's Economy
   A. Deficit
   B. Plans for Tax Hike
   C. Gambling Revenues to Offset Deficits

VI. Proposal
   A. Baltimore
      1. Unemployment
      2. Inner Harbor
      3. Compete with Atlantic City

VII. Conclusion

These are among the problems that you may have found in this outline:

- It is poorly arranged. Headings I and III are inconsistent. Note that Heading I suggests that Maryland has two forms of gambling—slot machines and casino nights—whereas Heading III adds an additional form: lotteries.

- It provides irrelevant information. Heading IV, Statistical Indicators, and Heading V, Maryland's Economy, may be related to this issue but only tangentially. They are extraneous to the immediate purpose of the paper.

- Headings are not placed according to the importance of subjects. Heading VI should appear early in the outline, since it contains the main or dominant purpose of the paper: to advocate legalization of casino gambling in Baltimore, thereby creating jobs in an area where unemployment is high.

Beginning to Write

Once you have prepared an outline, your prewriting stage will likely be over. This is the time to sit back and assess your provisional strategy (since that is what outlines really articulate). It is also a good time to retest certain ideas or arguments you have incorporated into the outline. Ask yourself if they are answerable or supportable by evidence, data, or research; if they are not, exclude them until you investigate further sources.

Finally, when you begin to write, keep in mind that your audience and purpose are always interconnected. Therefore, you must use that particular style, that particular strategy, and that particular voice that best serve that particular audience and purpose.

Writing within a Law Office

The preceding discussion covers the various kinds of audiences to which you will write. For those of you who are paralegals or legal interns working or planning to work in a law office, the following sections describe the kinds of writing that you will prepare *within* a law office.

Letters

This is the most common form of writing produced in law offices every day. Subjects of letters include the following:

- A letter requesting information
- A letter requesting payment
- A letter notifying that the office represents a person or company

There are more complicated letters that explain to a client the application of a particular law and to advise the client what to do. Such letters must present technical material in a clear, concise manner.

Formal Documents

Formal documents, in effect, do your work for you. Examples are contracts, deeds, wills, leases, bonds, notes, and mortgage agreements. You will seldom have to create a formal document in your own words. Rather, you will likely be provided a standard model that applies to your county, state, or jurisdiction, which will be adapted to the specific facts pertaining to the client.

Pleadings

Pleadings are simply those statements of claims or defenses submitted to the court that relate to the parties involved in litigation. The most common pleadings are the complaint, answer, counterclaim, reply to counterclaim, and, on occasion, the third-party complaint.

Briefs

There are several kinds of briefs that emanate from law offices. Their contents are generally arranged in this order: opening with the conclusion and then backing it up, focusing on the legal issue and the relevant law, explaining the law, applying the law to the case at hand, and delivering an emphatic conclusion.

Trial Brief

A trial brief is the set of notes written on how the attorney plans to present his or her case. The notes will include materials pertaining to the opening statement, witnesses' statements, exhibits to be produced, contents of direct and cross-examination, and the closing argument. In short, it contains the attorney's strategy.

Appellate Brief

An appellate brief is a formal argument directed to a court of appeals on why a lower court's decision should be affirmed, modified, or reversed. It is submitted to the appellate court and to the opposing side. The appellate brief is the most technical legal document produced by attorneys.

Sometimes a court will permit a nonparty to the litigations to submit an appellate brief, as well. This is known as a *Friend of the Court* or *Amicus Curiae* brief. It is allowed in circumstances whereby the appellate court believes that the nonparty will be affected in some way by the decision. The Friend of the Court brief generally states principles and legal advice on how the controversies of the case may be most judiciously resolved.

Memoranda

If you have done fairly extensive research on a legal issue, you may be required to write a memorandum of law that lays out your analysis.

Internal Memorandum

The audience for an internal memorandum is your supervisor or the attorney in charge of the case. It is the synthesis of your legal research. The primary features of an internal memorandum are its accuracy and thoroughness. It must anticipate questions and outcomes of any hearings or court proceedings that will take place with regard to the case.

External Memorandum

An external memorandum has an adversarial purpose—to persuade the reader to adopt a decision favorable to your client. It is less objective than the internal memorandum, since it emphasizes the weaknesses of the opposing party's position.

As you have seen, the different kinds of writing produced in a law office are directed to any number of audiences. Thus, the standards for reaching your audience, as outlined in this chapter, are equally applicable for these documents.

EXAMPLE 1.6 Law Office Letter

The following is an example of how to compose an elementary type of legal writing—the *Client Information Letter*—that you might be assigned as an intern or entry-level paralegal. It requires less knowledge of the law per se than do briefs. Law firms generally decide on their own styles of formats for correspondence, but they all incorporate these basic components in a letter to a client:

- An introductory paragraph providing the overall context of the letter
- An explanation of the pertinent issues involved, such as the client's legal rights, duties, and remedies
- A concluding section that may sum up matters or ask the client to take particular actions

The following example of a Client Information Letter incorporates the required basic components just itemized:

Law Office Heading

Ms. Andrea Brown

101 Maple Avenue

Yorktown Heights, NY 20456

Dear Ms. Brown:

At our meeting last week, you requested information regarding permanent residence or "Adjustment of Status" in order to avoid deportation orders. Our office advised you that deportation orders can be suspended if you comply with the legal standards that apply to a request for suspension of deportation.

These are the requirements you must meet. You must prove with notarized documentation that you have resided in the United

States for seven continuous years. Also, if you have a visa that was approved based on marriage to a U.S. citizen, and if you have secured employment based on visa status, you may be entitled to adjust your status to legal resident. Last, you must prove that you have been and still are a person of good moral character and that you have not violated the terms and conditions of your visa or work without authorization.

At our meeting last week, it seemed clear from your concerns about keeping your family intact that deportation would bring emotional hardship to both you and your family. We believe that obtaining suspension of a deportation order is possible. If you wish to proceed with this matter, we will have to discuss your situation and examine your visa and work documents carefully. Please make an appointment to meet with us and bring along these materials for our review.

Sincerely,

EXERCISES

1.1 *Analyzing Audience and Purpose*

1. Find an advertisement in a magazine or newspaper that appeals to one of the following types of audience: college students, computer buffs, homemakers, or senior citizens. Write several paragraphs about the ways this advertisement makes its appeal, especially in its use of language. Could it be improved? If so, how?

2. Look around your campus for graffiti. What kind of graffiti do you find? Where do you find it? Does it offer evidence of hostility toward a particular group (gender, race, religion, other)? Other than being used as a form of self-expression, does the graffiti have another purpose? Analyze.

3. Choose a proposed congressional bill on an issue of national importance (e.g., a federal highway bill). Name a set of different audiences that would be interested in such a bill (e.g., city dwellers and country dwellers). In a list of talking points for congressional lobbyists, specify the particular needs, and the best individual approaches to them, for each audience.

1.2 *Organizing an Opposing Team Outline*

Divide your class into several teams of four or five students each. Half of the teams will take a favorable position on an issue and half of the teams will take a negative position on the same issue. Then each team will prepare an outline, the contents and headings of which represent its position. Either side must target its argument to the same audience, as in the following example:

Issue: Should areas that contain endangered species be preserved by law or should owners have the right to build on these lands for economic gain?

Audience: A City Council considering passage of a preservation law

Suggestion: Pick examples that may be applicable to your own geographical location (i.e., shorefront property, wetlands, logging and forests, wilderness, etc.).

ENDNOTES

1. *Pyle By and Through Pyle v. South Hadley School Committee, Federal Supplement* (861) [1994].

2. *Tinker v. Des Moines Independent Community School District* (393 US 503 [1969]).

3. *Welfare Programs: Ineffective Federal Oversight Permits Costly Automated System Problems* (Washington, DC: General Accounting Office, Report to Congressional Requesters, GAO-IMTEC-92-29, May 1992).

4. Robert C. Kellner and Bradford W. Warbasse, "Testing for Drugs and Alcohol in the Workplace," *Maryland Bar Journal, XXVII* (November/December 1994): 21–22.

2

Legal Definition

You can best deliver a position in a legal document by providing clear, reliable definitions that are directly pertinent to your subject. Your ability to support positions with legal definitions promises a more professional, authoritative, and persuasive tone. Therefore, the purpose of this chapter is to provide answers to these two questions:

1. How and when should you define?
2. What are the different kinds of definitions you should use?

First, it is important to know your objective before deciding which legal definition(s) to select. You may, for example, be writing about recent debates regarding censorship on the Internet—a subject that promises to provoke interest in the twenty-first century. If you are writing to a legislator regarding an online business that is violating the Child Pornography Prevention Act of 1996, your definitions will necessarily be somewhat technical. They will involve classifications of terms that have appeared in previous related cases. Also, to further clarify your explanation, you may supplement these definitions with analogous legal phrases drawn from cases on pornography but not necessarily related to computer technology (e.g., some popular song lyrics).

On the other hand, if you are writing a memorandum to a local PTA director regarding Internet regulation and advocating how or whether families should manage this problem in their households, the precision of your definitions will be slightly different. The PTA director may not be familiar with the Child Pornography Prevention Act and its terminology or, for that matter, with recent child protection devices (e.g., NetNanny) for computers. Thus, you should begin with more elementary terms, such as "This act makes it a federal crime to depict, or appear to depict, children in sexually explicit conduct whether on film, computers, or still photographs."

Even the legislator may not be as acquainted with the material as you think. In that case, a simple review of definitions would be equally appreciated. It might also bring greater credence to your position, as well as acknowledgment of your professionalism. Thus, there are a number of factors to consider when you use legal definitions. The following guidelines will help you decide how and when to incorporate them into your writing.

Importance of Definition

The use of definitions becomes crucial when an issue is important in societal and political matters. The greater the number of citizens who may be affected, the more prominence and precision legal terms will require. Consider the subject of public safety in this hypothetical example.

A police officer passes a group of teenagers who are huddled on a street corner at night, speaking in low voices. Are they engaging in illegal behavior? Suppose the police officer believes that and disperses them; then suppose his action is called into question and requires a report. The officer must resort to a specific definition of what constitutes illegal loitering to justify his action by claiming "reasonable suspicion" that illegal action was taking place. In addition, factors such as the frequency of this particular nighttime practice, the number of teenagers present, and so on would enter into how the report substantiates an allegation of loitering. The text would focus on that part of the *loitering* definition that singles out an activity—for instance, soliciting or using drugs. Also, depending on what the officer actually witnessed, a definition of *reasonable suspicion* might be warranted. (Remember that such terms are readily available in the Federal or State Penal Code.)

Now take another example, this one factual. In 1992, at a New York City public school, a security guard noticed a bulge in the jacket of a student. The guard chased the student, reached inside the student's jacket, and removed a gun. This consequently resulted in the student being suspended from school. The episode created a tangle in the New York courts, since a definition of *reasonable suspicion* was the pivotal factor on both sides. Defined in one way, *reasonable suspicion* bolstered the teachers' and parents' demand for safety. Defined in such a way that no such suspicion seemed warranted, it operated to support a claim by the student for protection against "unreasonable search and seizure." The New York Court of Appeals ruled in favor of the student, creating even further dissent on the validity of applying this phrase. What is important in this discussion of legal definition is that in this case, the Appellate Court was exacting in its consideration of *reasonable suspicion,* citing definitions from earlier Supreme Court decisions that most closely resembled the circumstances of this case.

Moreover, the decision was qualified by the fact that school searches are generally governed by a different standard of reasonable suspicion than in places outside school settings. Nonetheless, a limitation built into the legal definition had bearing: The court determined that the guard lacked a specific "knowledge sufficient to induce an ordinarily prudent and cautious man under the circumstances to believe that criminal activity is at hand."[1] Thus, the first principle for supporting an argument through definition is to follow the example of the Appellate Court and find that definition that most closely relates to the circumstances of the case.

Tactics in Defining

Positioning Definitions

When considering your definitions, think about your strategy. You will not often write a definition merely to present information or explanations. Since your writing will be directed toward some hoped-for result, you will be asserting and arguing as well as defining. Also, since there are generally no fixed patterns for placement of your definitions, you should situate them with a sensitivity to your audience's attitude or predisposition. (Exceptions exist, of course, as when you are preparing a document that requires a standardized format, as in a contract or police report. In these instances, placement of definitions is more fixed and regulated.)

When addressing a resistant audience, it is sometimes good to forestall definitions and begin your document with a brief narrative. If you word a narrative *at* the audience—that is, you invite your readers to identify with an experience analogous to the events at hand—definitions can be more easily tolerated when they finally surface. Also, if your definition helps extend or strengthen your evidence, refer to it more than once in the document. This can be accomplished in various ways:

- Tag it onto your opening narrative.
- Repeat it when you cite reliable statistics or evidentiary facts.
- Apply it to circumstances that are unrelated to the present issue but that underscore the term's importance nevertheless.

Remember that legal definitions incorporated unobtrusively or in a subtle manner will prevent you from seeming strident or overly prejudicial. As another recommendation, especially when writing to a particularly sensitive audience, it may be beneficial to break down the definitions into parts, dispersing them in the text. This helps structure your argument while tying key elements of these definitions to particular aspects of the subject. Take, for example, the problem of the "English only" initiative, a legal matter that has recently surfaced as a result of the increasing diversity in the nation. Indeed, certain jurisdictions have already put in place their own versions of an "English only" policy.

Since this issue concerns the rights and privileges of a population of marked proportion, and since it figures in such vital matters as employment, primary authoritative definitions will be needed (e.g., definitions of those rights assured by the Constitution). In addition, there will be secondary definitions regarding the conditions under which these rights will be applicable (e.g., workplace practices where the rights of employers and of employees may come in conflict).

Regarding the issue of "English only," suppose that you are writing to the local Fair Employment Practices Commission on behalf of an immigrant who was fired for speaking his native language to another employee while on the job. The employer complained that this was jeopardizing business, since service and productivity were not delivered as satisfactorily or efficiently as she wished. This situation has ramifications on both sides: Employers (at least in private industry) have the right to advance their financial interests in a laissez-faire society; employees have the right to equal protection of the laws pertaining to freedom of speech (Amendment XIV). Legal definitions are mandatory here. They would include an assortment of terms, and, depending on the circumstances of the case, might even necessitate treatment of the term *discrimination.* Any appeal on the latter charge would have to demonstrate incorporation of such items in the definition of discrimination as "disparate treatment" to the employee. (These are defined in such federal statutes as Title VII of the Civil Rights Act of 1964, as amended.)

An accurate, objective statement of such a claim should give equal space and treatment to the defined rights of both the employer and the employee, since slighting one side of the case will automatically weaken the argument. How, then, would you incorporate legal definitions in this appeal regarding the employee's termination? Given the *when* and *how* tactics suggested earlier, you should (1) blend these definitions in with your narrative (a hard-working family suddenly gone hungry and homeless) and (2) strategically repeat legal phrases on rights accorded to both sides in rulings established in employment law (e.g., "business necessity," "disparate impact," etc.).

When is it advisable to use certain definitions? In the public domain, there are obvious agreed-upon definitions that may not need elaboration in your writing. These terms, which have been long entrenched in legal discourse (e.g., *burglary*), may be referred to as legal "terms of art," or "words that have a particular meaning to a particular area of study in law" (*Law Dictionary,* S. Gifis). However, there are other terms whose colorations and/or meanings have changed over time, generally as a result of the appearance of unprecedented types of behavior in criminal or civil cases. For example, *vigilantism*—in its traditional, folkloric sense—reminds many people of Wild West maneuvers and western movies, where it was often depicted as random lawlessness by marauders or bands of men existing outside established communities. Today, the term appears in courts with a decidedly different legal slant. Individuals acting alone, carrying weapons in metropolitan areas, who maim or murder suspected or actual accosters are being accused of *vigilantism.* Hence, the term now brings in formulated legal criteria that extend well beyond its traditional meaning (e.g., its significance when self-defense is the plea).

Thus, it is important to evaluate your management of definitions. Remember this important rule: Do not automatically presume that your audience understands the legal meanings of your terms. When in doubt, define.

Kinds of Definitions

There are various kinds of legal definitions and various methods of effectively providing them. Depending on your subject and audience, at times it might suffice to confine yourself to one definition; at other times it is prudent to load the text with numerous definitions. Discussion on the next several pages will focus on the basic and most frequently used kinds of definitions. As you will see, they vary in their hierarchy of purpose or importance. Also, notice that there is some inevitable overlap in them; kinds of definitions can serve more than one function at a time, forcing them to work in cross-reference. For example, of the nine categories of definition that will be discussed, the following three might be used if you are writing on the topic of *flag desecration:*

- *Definition by legal authority:* This would cite, for example, the United States Code Annotated, which enumerates the penalties for flag desecration.
- *Definition by example:* This would provide an instance of a particular act of flag desecration.
- *Definition by qualification:* This would indicate where such flag desecration may have taken place (e.g., in a public forum, during a political demonstration, etc.).

Definition by Legal Authority

In order to avoid confusion regarding definition by legal authority, keep in mind this distinction: Statutes, laws, codes, rulings—whether their source is judicial, executive, or legislative—are not definitions. However, they all contain definitions and remain the best resource for finding effective definitions. They are also the requisite documents for identifying (and dating) any revision, replacement, or interpretation of a definition that may occur.

An exact citation of a term or phrase promulgated by a governmental regulation weighs heavily in any criminal or civil matter. Use it as your standard for application. (See Chapter 6 for an annotated summary of the essential classifications of these documents.) For our purpose here, I will use the example of a current, much publicized legal issue: complaints filed that allege sexual harassment on the job. Claims appear as different charges and in different categories: (1) a woman accusing a particular individual at the office of "daily attempting to fondle me under the desk, although I kicked him away" and (2) a class-action suit brought by nearly 700 women employees at a Mitsubishi plant who claimed they were subject to constant groping, sexual graffiti, obscene language, and abusive comments by male coworkers and supervisors. Which of these satisfies an allegation of *sexual harassment?* The Equal Employment Opportunity Act (1972) enforces Title VII of the Civil Rights Act (1964). It provides the legal definition necessary to initiate a justification in either instance:

> Unwelcome sexual advances, requests for sexual favors and other verbal or physical conduct of a sexual nature constitute sexual harassment when (1) submission to such conduct is made either explicitly or implicitly a term or condition of an individual's employment; (2) submission to or rejection of such conduct by an individual is used as the basis for employment decisions affecting such individual; or, (3) such conduct has the purpose or effect of unreasonably interfering with an individual's work performance or creating an intimidating, hostile or offensive working environment.[2]

Clearly, the wording here would be as applicable to the isolated case as to the Mitsubishi corps of women. This is a statute where the stakes are high and deliberation depends on fair treatment of opposing parties; consequently, federal, state, and local rulings will remain your mandatory sources of definition.

Definition by Etymology and History

All legal terms have an etymology and a history; you might wish to include them when background information helps clarify certain ideas you are writing about. Perhaps you will want to use either one or both; in some instances, etymology and history are fused.

Etymology traces the origin and development of a term or phrase that has become part and parcel of legal usage. Some terms, such as *due process,* trace back centuries in U.S. law; others, such as *species,* have more recent beginnings and were brought into the lexicon for legal procedures that were nonexistent in earlier times (e.g., in connection with the Endangered Species Act).

History brings in the background of a term or phrase as it has operated in rulings and cases. Generally, when arguing cases, you will support an issue by giving a historical decision in which the term received a standard definition for arguing future cases (e.g., the *plain view* doctrine).

The influence of politically dominant forces or groups often determines what people are permitted to and prohibited from doing. These forces become the origin or occasion of major legal rulings and definitions, some of which date back to the writing of the Constitution. Indeed, the First Amendment's establishment of freedom of the press was focused on protecting against censorship those citizens who produced adversarial pamphlets and broadsheets during that turbulent period. This freedom accorded to the "press" has been broadened significantly, accommodating various forms of communication—nonexistent then but now grouped under an umbrella term: *the media.* Invoking the history of how events prompted creation of major laws gives you the foundation for arguing a current issue. In addition to recalling origins of such legal definitions, you can substantiate them further by citing contemporary interpretations. The most forceful of these interpretations are delivered by the Supreme Court.

One such legal definition, *gerrymandering,* which has currency today but had little effect in its time, originated with a ruling that took effect in 1812. Gerry Elbridge, governor of Massachusetts at the time, redistricted a geographical area known as Essex County. The area's figuration on a map resembled a salamander; hence the coupling of the ending of *salamander* and the governor's name gave us *gerrymander.*

The intention underlying this ruling was to give one political party a majority in as many electoral districts as possible; the result was to weaken the strength of a particular group at the advantage of those in power. Initially, the term *gerrymandering* was bandied about satirically, implying unfair manipulation. Today, the term is used frequently in the news and has assumed considerable importance during elections. Thus, bringing in its etymological and historical definition gives substance to a colloquialism.

Definition by Genus/Differentia

As with virtually all definitions, legal definitions carry several levels of classification. That is, they belong to a larger category or group of terms or topics and they contain qualities that distinguish them from other members of that category or group. The first category is known as *genus;* the second is known as *differentia.* For example, under the genus of *major economic crimes,* you will find *bribery* as a differentia; the differentia specifies bribery as that act by which one person tries to persuade the judgment of another by the offer of money. However, the definitions for *graft* and *extortion* are different from that for *bribery;* yet they are two other differentia that fall under the same genus as bribery (i.e., major economic crimes).

The genus/differentia distinction isolates and refines your definition, helping you avoid generalizations. Consider the various differentia for the genus term *abuse:* They are differentiated by method, as in physical abuse, emotional abuse, sexual abuse, verbal abuse, and so on. Likewise, consider the subset of differentia that fall under these categories, such as differentiation by subject of abuse, as in spousal abuse, child abuse, or animal abuse. Each has separate compartmental criteria that are relegated to even narrower subsets of differentia. For example, there is a difference between physically hurling your dog out of the house and doing the same to your 3-year-old child. While each has placement under the larger heading of abuse, the action toward the 3-year-old is a violation of that passage of the Domestic Violence Act that states the following actions: "(1) to cause bodily harm, (2) to place another in fear of imminent serious bodily harm."[3] Domestic violence is a differentia applicable to family members, not to a dog. (For that matter, laws against killing humans do not apply to animals, as in slaughterhouses.)

Definition by Example

The most common way to define in ordinary communication is to provide examples or illustrations of what you wish to convey. These examples convert abstractions or obscure meanings into realistic representations. This is also the case with legal definitions, especially when the examples are directly targeted and are close in time, circumstance, and function to the meaning you wish to convey. Any newspaper reader can toss out examples of terms frequently used in legal writing. An attorney might use a phrase such as *change of venue* in a pleading to the court. However, an example of this procedure in another case can fortify your argument, so long as you select the right case.

Also, depending on your audience, it might be necessary to explain how the change of geographic location for the trial in your example reflects circumstances similar to the trial discussed in your text (e.g., if yours is a civil trial, use another civil trial rather than a criminal trial). The problems requiring change of venue would be different for each. In a case that involves charges against a bank president whose embezzlement of funds has destroyed the savings of a large segment of the community, the district court judge might determine that a change of venue is necessary to ensure an unprejudiced jury.

As another example, suppose there is an industrial corporation whose contaminant runoffs have widely polluted the drinking water in a community, causing health problems. Here, too, the judge orders a change of venue for the trial. In both instances, you would need to find examples appropriate and analogous to the issues. Citing a sensational murder or terrorist trial in which change of venue also was ordered would be irrelevant and even counterproductive to your argument.

Definition by Issue

In the practice of law, an *issue* is "a single, certain and material point, deduced by the allegations and pleadings of the parties, which is affirmed on the one side, and denied on the other; a fact put in controversy by the pleadings; such may either be issues of law or fact. An 'issue' is a disputed point or question to which parties to action have narrowed their several allegations and upon which they are desirous of obtaining either a decision of court on question of law or of court or jury on question of fact" (*Black's Law Dictionary,* 5th Edition).

Therefore, application of this form of definition becomes important when the nature of a problem is in contention with another contingent definition. For example, bicycles are lumped together with motorcycles, cars, and trucks as vehicular modes of transportation. Unlike laws regarding motorcycles, cars, and trucks, however, there is no requirement that a bicycle owner get a license or pass a driver's test. Yet there have been recent cases where bikers who were considered drunk were charged with driving under the influence (DUI). Thus, in the case of the bicycle, this vehicle is defined differently according to which issue is relevant. When the issue is citation for a DUI, the bicycle is classified with motorcycles, cars, vans, trucks, and so forth. When the issue is the requirement for an operator's license, then the bicycle is put in the class of roller skates, wagons, surfboards, and other recreational paraphernalia for which no license is required.

Let's try another hypothetical example. Suppose you are writing an initiative for a civic association that requests that the street on which a former sex molester has just established residence be placed on 24-hour police patrol. How would definition by issue be applicable here? The citizens argue that this resident is potentially dangerous and that immediate cooperation from the police district is in order. The law-enforcement officials claim that neighborhood monitoring is in full effect already and that funding for this patrol would be diverted from detailing personnel to other areas, such as crack-house sites. Moreover, such surveillance might actually qualify as invasion of this molester's privacy rights.

This example has compelling implications for both sides and must be expressed through definitions linked to the citizens' initiative. When the issue for the civic association is *protection,* legally defined as "to preserve in safety; to keep intact" (i.e., the citizens had dwelt in this neighborhood in relative safety before this new development), and when the police department's issue is the possibility of liability for *invasion of privacy* (i.e., privacy of the molester), then *proper surveillance* enters the terminology—but is used differently by either side. For the citizens, proper surveillance means round-the-clock police presence on that street; for the police department, proper surveillance means that type of surveillance that will not impinge on one person's privacy.

Definition by Negation

One technique for eliminating unwarranted complications in legal writing is to stipulate what is not germane to your argument. It is easy to be enticed by dramatic terminology, but you must establish your claim with appropriate language. This determines what definitions you will select and how they omit or negate other inapplicable terms. An often confused pair of terms, *beating* and *battering,* illustrates this. Although beating may constitute a part of the battering that occurs in a domestic violence case, it is not battering. The former refers to a single incident in which physical injury has resulted. The latter refers to repeated abuse that assumes different forms (physical, verbal, emotional, etc.). This explains why we know of shelters for *battered* women rather than for *beaten* women.

Consider the kind of claims made by people who feel they have been subjected to unwarranted censorship. A legal battle that ultimately landed in the Supreme Court in 1986 over a Bethel, Washington, school's disciplinary action is a good illustration of such litigation. A student made a speech nominating another student for elective office. The nature of the speech prompted the school to punitive action, which was to suspend the student from school for a brief period and to bar him from delivering a commencement speech. Here is part of the student's speech:

> I know a man who's firm—he's firm in his pants, he's firm in his shirt, his character is firm—but most of all, his belief in you, the students of Bethel, is firm. Jeff Kuhlman is a man who takes his point and pounds it in. If necessary, he'll take an issue and nail it to the wall. He doesn't attack things in spurts—he drives hard, pushing and pushing until finally—he succeeds. Jeff is a man who will go to the very end—even the climax—for each and every one of you.[4]

The momentum of this case derived from the student's charge that his discipline was a form of censorship. The Supreme Court ruled in favor of the school officials, denying that the school's punishment called forth the question of censorship or First Amendment protection. Writing for the majority in this decision, Chief Justice Burger argued, "Nothing in the Constitution prohibits the states from insisting that certain modes of expression are inappropriate and subject to sanctions." Rather, Burger said that the student had violated Bethel High School's disruptive-conduct rule prohibiting the use of obscene language "which substantially interferes with the educational process."[5]

Thus, by negating any question of free speech, the school was able to win. Instead, they resorted to a carefully limited charge of "disruptive conduct." Using this charge, they offered the teachers' personal testimonies that their instructional schedules were interrupted in order to address students' reactions to the episode.

This decision by the Supreme Court applied to a rule in which forms of speech are forbidden in certain forums and for certain cogent reasons. For instance, a person cannot as a capricious antic shout "Fire!" in a crowded theater without the danger of incurring legal consequences. Thus, while definition by negation seldom requires extensive analysis, it is important to state what is not being contested. In short, you must decide *exactly* what justification your definitions have on the subject.

Definition by Operation

An *operational definition* is one that can be acted on. It provides the criterion for judging a particular situation and, in the process, permits the creation of limitations. Use of the operational definition abounds in legal writing, since so many litigational matters turn on what is permissible behavior. Apply this to the Fourth Amendment, which on many occasions is used to determine whether a particular police activity is deemed an unreasonable search. The definition of *search* inevitably leads back to this segment of the Fourth Amendment: "The right of the people to be secure in their persons, houses, papers, and effects, against unreasonable searches and seizures, shall not be violated."

Written to protect people from government intrusion into their privacy and the sanctity of their homes, this search clause has become increasingly problematic due to technology. Instances of cases where the operational interpretation of *search* was questioned include (1) government agents flying at a low altitude over a citizen's backyard to determine if he is growing marijuana;[6] (2) police noting the serial number underneath a stereo (suspecting stolen goods) while in someone's house for unrelated but legitimate reasons;[7] and (3) government agents placing a beeper in a car so that agents can track it.[8]

Clearly, cars did not exist in the eighteenth century, making it necessary to establish by case law whether the Fourth Amendment's protection regarding "houses" is applicable—or, for that matter, whether a person's backyard constitutes part of his or her house. In two of these cases (the agents' aerial observation to search for possible marijuana plants and hiding a beeper in a car so that it could be tracked), neither of which involved entry into a house proper, the Court found that the agents had not violated the so-called search clause. However, regarding the case in which police noted a serial number under a stereo, the reverse was claimed.

What was the difference? In the instance of the serial number, the police had a warrant for entry into the house, but the stereo number, being underneath the appliance, was not in "plain view." Here, the Court qualified the operational definition of *search* according to the degree of scrutiny that was deemed allowable.

Definition by Description

Description is one of the more literal ways to write legal definitions. Here, technical or obscure terminology gives way to explanation of terms as they are put into effect by the legal system. These definitions bring in factual details that are necessary to explain a process, a component of the criminal justice system, a legal procedure, and so on. For example, defining *DNA* requires giving the description of a genetic formula that controls a human being's biological makeup. Its description is interrelated with its function in legal matters—to verify evidence in the physiological makeup (e.g., blood type, hair sampling, etc.) of individuals.

A definition by description also tells what the process or action in question does or is supposed to accomplish. For example, Drug Court is a recent type of judicial structure that was created to process illegal substance cases for the purpose of reducing caseloads in the regular court system. Another objective of Drug Court is to better manage nonviolent substance-abuse offenders by focusing on their treatment rather than on serving them jail sentences. Thus, the description of such a court and its actions would enumerate such considerations as the following: (1) eligibility (e.g., the offender must not have a firearm in possession at time of arrest); (2) supervision of the offender (e.g., random testing); and (3) the offender's successful completion of a treatment-oriented program as ordered by the court.

Definition by description of a term may also include consideration of particular groups that are affected by it. So-called hate crimes, for example, are defined by identifying the groups that are vulnerable to these crimes, the areas in which the crimes take place, and the frequency of those crimes. Also, such crimes are often committed in a form of symbolic degradation, represented by objects (e.g., burning crosses), graphic markings (e.g., swastikas), and vandalism (e.g., property defilement). These different and qualifying means of enacting hate crimes are therefore part of the construct of this definition.

The persuasiveness of definition by description consequently brings to bear the practical consequences of an issue or problem. They formulate the *what, how,* and *who* of a particular legal subject.

Standard Legal Usage Definitions

Most professions have certain terms whose meanings differ from their usage in everyday parlance. In medicine, for example, the term *invasive* indicates a medical procedure that involves penetrating the body (e.g., tonsillectomy). In common usage, *invasive* has wide connotations, ranging from anything adversarial to actual military activities. The same is true of legal terminology, where certain terms assume specialized meanings distinct from their meanings in other forms of writing. (As noted earlier in this chapter, in the field of law, these terms are known as *terms of art.*) It is necessary, especially for lay readers, to clarify terms as they operate specifically in legal practice. Consider these examples:

- *Discovery:* This is often associated with a unique advance or progress in history—scientific, geographic, or spatial. However, the legal definition for *discovery* is the "pretrial procedures by which the parties to a lawsuit obtain information from other parties and from potential witnesses. . . . Discovery provisions also safeguard against unwarranted intrusions into the opponent's files" (*Law Dictionary,* S. Gifis).

- *Material:* This word describes any number and species of objects. People speak of building material, material used in scholarly journals, and so on. But in the field of law, *material* is defined as that which is "important, necessary; relating to a given matter, and relevant evidence which tends to prove or disprove any ultimate issue." One such use of the term is *material witness* (*Law Dictionary*, S. Gifis).

- *Contempt:* This word, in common usage, refers to an attitude expressed or felt toward individuals or their actions. Its legal definition, on the other hand, consists of several classifications of liability—direct contempt, constructive contempt, civil contempt, or criminal contempt. Yet, for all of these classifications, the term *contempt* conforms to a broader definition as "an act or omission tending to obstruct or interfere with the orderly administration of justice" (*Law Dictionary*, S. Gifis).

Interpreting Definitions

The plot thickens. Earlier sections of this chapter had to do with the placement and construction of definitions, but as you have seen, definitions do not always resolve or clarify the meanings we intend in legal writing. Because definitions are created through language, which changes in usage over time, and because definitions become refined through an evolution of laws and court decisions, interpretation becomes challenging. For example, the Eighth Amendment's prohibition against cruel and unusual punishment is continually being interpreted and reinterpreted. New case law contributes new definitions, which in turn necessitate even further interpretation. Often, these interpretations are generated and forced by sociocultural and political contexts. That process can be seen in the following two examples.

EXAMPLE 2.1 Interpretation of First Amendment Rights in *Texas v. Johnson* (1989)

This case centered on flag desecration, which has a checkered history of interpretation in the United States. Cases dealing with this issue involve the statutory restrictions placed on desecration (e.g., mutilating, defacing, defiling, burning, or trampling upon) and the constitutional question regarding free or symbolic speech. These cases pit the government's interest in protecting the physical integrity of the U.S. flag against those individuals who see desecration as a vehicle for expressing political opinions, as guaranteed by the First Amendment. Political demonstrators, for instance, often assert that flag burning expresses patriotism rather than the reverse.

One case that exemplifies interpretation of freedom of speech pertains to a public flag burning during the 1984 Republican Convention in Dallas, Texas. Gregory Johnson, who doused a flag with kerosene and set it on fire, was charged with "desecration of a venerated object," found guilty, and sentenced to prison. A reversal of the conviction by the Texas Court of Criminal Appeals brought an appeal from the state of Texas to the U.S. Supreme Court, which decided in favor of Johnson.

The purpose here is not to discuss the particulars of the decision, which included interpretations of additional charges associated with the burning, such as "breach of the peace." Rather, the purpose is to focus on the different ways the court interpreted the term *free speech*. In the decision, *speech* progressively became variably interpreted as an expression or expressive. First, Johnson's conduct was designated as "symbolic speech," since it took place in an organized demonstration and, in this context, his action was seen as an integral part of that demonstration. (Here, his action was labeled *expression*.) Then it was determined that the burning constituted "expressive conduct," sufficiently imbued with elements of communication to fall within the scope of the First and Fourteenth Amendments. Since the flag itself was held to be "pregnant with expressive content," Johnson's use of the flag for a political message must also have "expressive elements."

The text of the decision then returned to the term *free speech* by recognizing that a principal "function of free speech under our system of government is to invite dispute." However, Johnson's "expressive conduct" did not fall within the class of "fighting words"—here defined as "likely to provoke the average person to retaliation." Finally, the Court held that Johnson's action did not communicate a message related to "the suppression of free expression," but rather to its opposite.[9]

EXAMPLE 2.2 The Kente Case Interpretation

The second example of interpretation by definition is an offshoot of the legal problems that continue to complicate the definition of *free speech*. This involves a situation that took place in the Washington, DC,

Superior Court in June 1992. An attorney representing a defendant charged with assault and intent to murder appeared in court wearing an African-style kente stole over his suit. The judge ordered the attorney to remove the stole, claiming that it might unfairly prejudice a jury in favor of him and his client, both of whom were African Americans. (It should be noted that, given the trial's location in a DC court, the jurors were predominantly African Americans.) The attorney refused to comply, claiming the order infringed on his free speech rights. The judge consequently removed him from the case, whereupon the attorney filed a petition in the DC Court of Appeals, asking that the judge either lift his ban or recuse himself as judge for not being impartial. The issue had further interpretative ramifications regarding the First Amendment, since the stole was a cultural symbol. Interpretations abounded, fueled by prominent newspaper coverage, editorials, and countereditorials.

An editorial in the *Washington Post* sided with the attorney, arguing that the judge's claim that the presence of the stole might cause the jury to lose judgment and objectivity was a flagrant insult to the jury's intelligence.[10] In a rejoinder, former Supreme Court Justice Warren Burger submitted a counteropinion to the *Washington Post,* arguing that freedom of speech was not the issue here. He noted that since time immemorial, dress codes for ceremonial and other public proceedings have been part of every society. Referring to court procedures in particular, Burger exclaimed, "What a bizarre business it would be for a Knight of Columbus to appear with his elegant, military-style garb and flowered hat, and perhaps the sword. If a kente cloth is permissible, why not the same rule for Knights of Columbus?"[11]

Burger's interpretation held that this claim of First Amendment protection was invalid, since it would obstruct or interfere with the orderly administration of justice. Concomitant with this is the inherent power of courts to prescribe standards of personal appearance and attire in a courtroom. The emphasis on court-imposed rules added another dimension to free speech interpretation, which is sure to be reinterpreted in future events with analogous policy circumstances.

The examples of flag desecration and the episode involving the kente stole demonstrate the wide applications and interpretations of legal definitions. Thus, there is a standard whereby *free speech* is defined as a form of verbal expression. This moves outward, with *free speech* being redefined as a form of symbolic action. The term becomes further extended to include the wearing of certain attire, which must consider *where* attire as "free speech" is constitutionally guaranteed. As new cases appear, other interpretations will undoubtedly arise.

EXERCISES

Here are five hypothetical problems. Write an answer for each one. Each problem is accompanied by one or more sources of legal definitions. In your answer, discuss (1) whether the definition is applicable to the problem and (2) if applicable, how it supports your answer.

2.1 *Interpreting Probable Cause*

A group of neighborhood citizens goes to law officials to report about a local resident whom they strongly suspect of defacing their property, painting graffiti on their cars, and placing notes containing racial slurs in their mailboxes. This person has been seen constantly visiting the video rental store. The police detective believes that the kinds of films the individual rents may provide evidence of his culpability. Does the detective have *probable cause* to request this person's rental record from the store?

Sources: (1) The Video Protection Act of 1988 provides for civil actions against rental businesses for disseminating or divulging a customer's history of film rental (*Business Law,* Barron's Educational Series, Inc.). (2) One ruling emanating from the Fourth Amendment regarding probable cause to search is that (a) "the specific items to be searched for are connected with criminal activity and (b) that these items will be found in the place to be searched."

2.2 *Justifying Search and Seizure*

John LaGrange owns a 30-acre farm on which he raises produce, both for family consumption and for sale at a stand fronting his property. A neighbor tells a police officer that she is sure part of that acreage is devoted to growing marijuana, since there is an unusual scent emanating from the farm on breezy evenings. Do law officials have the authority to search Mr. LaGrange's property?

Sources: (1) The Fourth Amendment protects the "right of people to be secure in their persons, houses, papers and effects against unreasonable searches." (2) In 1961, a "curtilage clause" provided further protection with regard to that part of the Amendment that defines *houses* in the following way: "All buildings in close proximity to a dwelling, which are continually used for carrying on domestic employment, or such place as is necessary and convenient to a dwelling, and is habitually used for family purposes" (*U.S. v. Potts,* 297 F.2d 68, 6th Cir.).

2.3 *Claiming Breaking and Entering*

Joe Santos had been fired from his brick-layer job because his boss had no work. As a result, Joe was evicted from his apartment for failing to meet rent payment; therefore, Joe slept in public parks. During a storm, he ran into an alley, where he saw an appliance store window whose glass had been removed for repair. He climbed through the window and spent the night in the store. The next morning, the store owner found Joe and called the police, demanding his arrest for breaking and entering. Does the store owner have grounds for this demand?

Source: "'Breaking and Entering' are two of the elements necessary to constitute a burglary. . . . It may be any act of physical force, however slight, by which obstruction to an entrance is removed. For example, the pushing open of a door that is ajar followed by entrance into a building will be sufficient to constitute the 'breaking and entering' elements of burglary" (*Law Dictionary,* S. Gifis).

2.4 *Withholding Information*

Jim Benson discovers through an inter-office memo that the corporation for which he works plans to build a research facility on a large piece of property that is uncultivated or fallow. The corporation plans to offer competitive, development prices if the owner agrees to sell. Jim contacts Lois Standwell, the owner, and offers to purchase the land, claiming that he wants to raise horses on it, since grazing land would be seen as commanding more modest prices than property for corporation expansion.

He does not tell Lois about the memo. Lois sells Jim the land just days before the corporation, unaware of the purchase, makes her an offer. Could an argument be made here for fraud?

Source: Fraud is the "intentional misrepresentation of a material fact made knowingly, with intent to defraud, that is justifiably relied upon by the other party and causes injury to the other party" (*Business Law,* Barron's Educational Series, Inc.).

2.5 *Validating Wills*

Sally Rosen owns a business that she has promised to leave, upon her retirement, to the man who served as her manager for 20 years. Sally dies suddenly, leaving a will that is valid according to the statutes in her state. As designated in this will, Sally's daughter takes over the business, which is included as part of the mother's estate. The manager claims that his boss told him she would adjust her will. In addition, the manager provides proof that he turned down more lucrative job opportunities because of Sally's longstanding promise. Does the manager have standing to sue the daughter?

Source: A *will* is "an instrument executed by a testator or testatrix according to the formalities required by state statute, setting forth how that person's estate is to be distributed after his/her death." Included among the requirements are (a) "that the will be in writing, (b) that it be made by someone who is an adult of sound mind, and (c) that it be signed by the testator/testatrix in the presence of two or three witnesses" (*Business Law,* Barron's Educational Series, Inc.).

ENDNOTES

1. "Keeping Guns Out of School," *The New York Times,* September 21, 1996, Editorial Section, p. 18.
2. Equal Employment Opportunity Act of 1972, 42 U.S.C. §2000e (1976).
3. *Maryland Domestic Violence Act,* §4-504 (1980).
4. *Bethel v. Fraser,* 478 U.S. 675 (1986).
5. Ibid.
6. *California v. Ciraolo,* 476 U.S. 207 (1986).
7. *U.S. v. Knotts,* 460 U.S. 276 (1983).

8. *Arizona v. Hicks*, 480 U.S. 321 (1987).

9. *Texas v. Johnson*, 491 U.S. 397 (1989).

10. "Judging the Kente Cloth," *The Washington Post,* June 13, 1992, Editorial Section, p. A20.

11. Warren Burger, "The Kente Case," *The Washington Post,* June 16, 1992, Editorial Section, p. A23.

3

Style in Legal Prose

> *Style* is a slippery word.
>
> *Style* is a semantic ambiguity, a linguistic conundrum, replete with a panoply of applications.

These two sentences, in themselves, represent how styles can differ. The first is a simple statement, suggesting that the word is hard to precisely define; the second suggests the same, but in more complex terminology. When thinking of style, we might make associations such as the Dior style in fashion, Picasso's style in painting, and Michael Jordan's style as a sports personality. However, this chapter treats *style* as it is used in forms of legal prose—as a clear, factual, concise way of writing that is intended to inform and persuade.

Legal prose deals with writing related to day-to-day activities, from a routine traffic law to trial proceedings for a vehicular damage suit. Yet, whatever the document or its purpose, its principles of style remain the same. This chapter will identify those principles that are fundamental to effective legal writing—from microlevels, such as the elements of sentence design, to macrolevels, such as paragraph organization and the total structure of the text.

The Sentence Level

Sentence Styles

You probably recall reading literary works dating from the nineteenth century in which the sentences were overlong, such as this one from Henry Thoreau's *Walden:*

> I went to the woods because I wished to live deliberately, to front only the essential facts of life, and see if I could learn what it had to teach, and not, when I came to die, discover that I had not lived.

This sentence is written in the *hypotactic* style. You may not be familiar with this grammatical term (which means to subordinate one clause or construction to another), but it is apparent that the sentence has several clauses that separate the main subject and predicate (*I went to the woods*) from its final verb clause, which emphasizes what Thoreau wished to avoid by going to Walden (*discover that I had not lived*). The clauses in between qualify and delay the total idea (e.g., *to live deliberately*), creating a kind of suspense and building up reasons for an effective climax.

Then, too, you may have read a story by Ernest Hemingway ("Big Two-Hearted River") where you found passages such as this:

> Nick had one good trout. He did not care about getting many trout. Now the stream was shallow and wide. There were trees along both banks. The trees of the left bank made short shadows on the current in the forenoon sun.

This style, generally written in declarative sentences that are set down successively or in series, is known as *paratactic.* Unlike compound or complex sentences normally found in a hypotactic style, these sentences tend to be shorter and grammatically simpler.

Both styles have their place in good legal prose, when used appropriately. For example, try to avoid long sentences so clogged with subordinate clauses that they risk unintelligibility. At the same time, try to avoid stringing together sentences so slight in content that they should be combined into one sentence as a fully formulated idea. The best strategy for refining your style is to vary the kinds of sentences; give your reader a "breather" intermittently. That is, after writing a dense passage, or when you wish to be emphatic, bring in short sentences for the punch.

Finally, when choosing sentence lengths and styles, always be sure of your audience's level of comprehensibility. If you are preparing documents that are used by the average citizen—such as tax forms, contracts, or benefit claims—it is best to keep sentences simple, with everyday meanings. (I will speak later of instances where a more complex style is preferred.)

Word Choice

When writing sentences, choose your vocabulary carefully and eliminate unnecessary words. Direct, clear writing keeps your readers attentive; bloated, obscure word usage makes readers spend time untangling the meaning (perhaps with annoyance), thereby distracting them from processing the actual subject matter. Consider this sentence:

> While the exacerbation of the uninsured motorist will indubitably be ameliorated by the Mandatory Insurance Act, the experience of other jurisdictions with compulsory insurance statutes instructs us that this problem cannot be alleviated by the Act.

This could be pared down to a shorter, clearer sentence:

> Jurisdictions with similar statutes indicate that the Mandatory Insurance Act may lessen, but probably not solve, the uninsured motorist problem.

Effective word choice is not just confined to avoiding inflated diction. It also means knowing when to use the right pronouns and when to select the right word for a compelling message. The following sentences deliver the same message:

1. We have nothing to fear but fear itself.
2. Stop being scared of yourself!
3. The only thing we have to conquer is our own fear.
4. There is nothing to be afraid of except being afraid.

You may recognize Sentence 1 as a famous quote from Franklin D. Roosevelt's Inaugural Speech in 1933. Why is it still quoted with some reverence? Some background on this may help.

Roosevelt made this speech at the height of the Depression; he was urging the nation to unite in overcoming a great economic crisis. Note that he did not use the pronoun *you* but the collective pronoun *we;* with the mere choice of a pronoun, he succeeded in rallying himself with all Americans. Moreover, he did not imply that the citizenry were afraid, as in Sentence 4; rather, he used *fear*—a more abstract, hence more remote, word—to suggest that it is not part of the nation's psyche. Also, Roosevelt did not deliver an order, as seen in the imperative Sentence 2, nor did he resort to the word *scared,* a level of usage surely ill-fitted for an Inaugural Address.

Word choice can alter the effectiveness of a text even in the selection of such simple parts of speech as articles (*a, an, the,* etc.). Consider how significant word choice is in the following:

1. In the beginning was *the* Word.
2. It all began with *a* Word.

Sentence 1 (John 1:1), with the definite article *the,* carries the sort of authority one expects from the Bible. In Sentence 2, the indefinite article *a* lacks that authoritative force.

Thus, selecting the exact word in legal writing not only enhances your style but it also strengthens your meaning. Often, when you are tempted to write a phrase when one word will suffice, write just the one (e.g., *may* for *is entitled to, think* for *of the opinion that, because* for *because of the fact that,* etc.).

Word Associations

Words are powerful little engines! They not only convey their denoted meanings (i.e., explicit meanings) but they also convey connoted meanings (i.e., suggested meanings). For example, the word *judge* explicitly *denotes* the presiding officer in a courtroom situation. The word also *connotes* fairness, power, and wisdom. (Think of famous trials in recent years that you have either read about or watched on television. The judges were given considerable media exposure. Isn't it fair to say that your impression of them was suffused—whether positively or negatively—with the connotations just mentioned?) Therefore, it is important to use words with an awareness of their connotative as well as denotative forces.

Here is an example of very strong connotations associated with word choice. Among the many loaded statements made between adversaries in the highly publicized Clinton–Lewinsky investigation, Monica Lewinsky's attorney, William Ginsburg, claimed that Independent Counsel Kenneth Starr's actions toward his client "may have ravaged the life of a youngster."[1] Whether or not Ginsburg's statement is a melodramatic call for sympathy for his client, his word choice clearly connotes Starr's ruthless treatment of Lewinsky.

The following list is a sample of words that frequently appear in legal discourse. Note that those words in Column 1 carry less negative weight than those in Column 2:

Column 1	*Column 2*
charge	crime
offense	transgression
offender	criminal
reconstruction	lie
debate	disagreement
fame	notoriety
opposition	enemy
power	intimidation
control	coercion

In common usage, the words in Column 2 tend to have stronger emotive—and connotative—force than do those in Column 1. Thus, while it will be appropriate at times to use the words in Column 2, they should accurately and fairly express the meanings you intend to communicate.

Noninflammatory Language

Consider these two statements about the Republican party:

> The Republican party greedily sneaks through the Congress devious legislative schemes that rob the hard-working middle class in order to wrongly benefit the ultra-rich.

> A popular distinction between Republican and Democratic legislation holds that the Republican party fosters those types of laws the first benefits of which are largely to the business community. This is in order that such stimulation of production will eventually benefit the wage earner.

In effect, both statements are making a similar claim: The Republican party supports the kind of legislation in which business profits. However, the first statement is loaded with inflammatory words, often heard or read during political campaigns. The second statement uses generally accepted technical terms that avoid the heavy connotations of such words in the first statement as *greedily, devious,* and *ultra-rich.*

Thus, while many politicians are known to distort language for various purposes, remember that writers of legal prose should aspire to higher, more ethical standards.

Metaphors

As humans, we have considerable skill in communicating through symbolic language, especially with the use of metaphors. In legal writing, use of metaphor can heighten style and give a memorable effect to a text that would ordinarily contain dry, literal discourse. However, metaphor must be used with care. It must embellish rather than obscure meaning, and it must serve a practical rather than ornamental purpose in the text.

Here is an instance of metaphoric usage by a Pennsylvania Supreme Court Justice who dissented in a case, claiming that the court interfered with the collective bargaining process. The judge began his overall metaphor with a simile (using the word *like*) related to baseball and then in the last sentence delivered his metaphor:

> [The Court Majority] adds a limitation which is like saying that a ball player has the right to bat for his team, but requiring that he stand at the plate without a bat. . . . The Majority here fails to see what the ball game is about.[2]

The most important rules regarding metaphors are not to mix them and not to use figurative phrases that make the point in a strained fashion. Here is an example:

> This world is in grave danger of becoming the victim of a general recession.

Can the world become a victim? (That is, is it effective to personify the abstract noun *world* by using the concrete noun *victim?*) Also, what about the adjective *grave* in *grave danger*—is it an unintentional pun? Indeed, the metaphor, although mixed, might work better if the sentence warned of the danger of a nuclear holocaust rather than of a recession—a far less ominous prospect.

If you use a metaphor in a document, it is a good idea to echo or retain it throughout the text rather than to incorporate different ones. For example, William Bennett, often called the "drug czar" of President George Bush's administration, published an article in *Reader's Digest* (March 1990), in which he denounced certain political figures who advocate drug legalization. He began the essay:

> Since I took command of the war on drugs, I have learned from former Secretary of State George Shultz that our concept of fighting drugs is "flawed."

(Shultz had advocated legalization of marijuana.) Bennett then proceeded in the article to defend his reasons for keeping drugs illegal. But in closing, he reverted to the *war* metaphor:

> Imagine if, in the darkest days of 1940, Winston Churchill had rallied the West by saying, "This war looks hopeless, and besides, it will cost too much. Hitler can't be *that* bad."

For the people who read *Reader's Digest,* many of whom can recall World War II, this metaphor made Bennett's message more compelling.

Finally, a word is needed about a second cousin (not highly regarded) to the metaphor: the cliché. Some clichés originated as vital metaphors that, through overuse, lost their effectiveness (e.g., *take up the cudgel, grist to the mill,* etc.); some are expressions that have become trite and meaningless due to overuse (e.g., *in these troubled times, the hard-earned dollar,* etc.). George Orwell gave us a witty rule of thumb about clichés: "Never use a metaphor, simile or other figure of speech which you are used to seeing in print" ("The Language and Symbols of Politics"). In other words, avoid stale language.

Prepositional Phrases

The prepositional phrase, a grammatical form that writers often (perhaps too often) resort to, can clutter a legal writing style unless it is used sparingly. The following sentence (discussed earlier in the section on metaphor) is faulty not only because of its awkward metaphor but also because of its string of prepositional phrases:

> This world is *in* grave danger *of* becoming the victim *of* a general recession.

Prepositional phrases make for wordiness and tend to slow down the progress of ideas in a sentence. For example, which of these sentences makes the point more effectively?

1. The meaning of a statement inheres in the method of making that statement.
2. The medium is the message.

Sentence 2 is from Marshall McLuhan's *Understanding Media* (1964), in which he argues that the means of communication (i.e., the medium) has a greater influence than the message itself. His taut sentence delivers the same meaning as Sentence 1, but in fewer words—and without prepositional phrases.

Another rule to observe when using prepositional phrases is to keep them as close to their modifiers as possible—for example:

1. The prosecutor observed that the photograph was found to be falsified in Demonstration #2 of the evidence.
2. The prosecutor observed, from the Demonstration #2 evidence, that the photograph was falsified.

Sentence 2 clarifies where the photograph was falsified; in Sentence 1, it is not clear whether Demonstration #2 had falsified the evidence or that the photograph had already been falsified.

To be sure, there are instances of prepositional phrases for which we will always be grateful. In his Gettysburg Address, Abraham Lincoln delivered a moving and memorable example when he spoke of our government "*of* the people, *by* the people, and *for* the people." These three prepositions are like pedestals for the phrase parallels and word repetition.

Active versus Passive Voice

The English sentence has the following basic grammatical structure: a subject, a verb, and an object. Every grammar handbook tells you this. The handbook may also give you a formula for writing a basic sentence using the (preferred) active voice. The pattern is *Who* does *what* to *whom?* as in the following:

> The judge sentenced the defendant.

This sentence, when written in the passive voice, would read something like this:

> The sentence for the defendant was delivered by the judge.

What is the difference? In the second sentence, the strong verb *sentenced* is weakened to a noun (*sentence*) in the grammatical process known as *nominalization.* As a result, the second sentence needs more words in order to be understood.

In legal prose, the active voice carries more weight and emphasis. However, there will be occasions when this rule will not apply. For example, if the person performing the action in a sentence is unknown or unimportant, then the passive voice should be used. For instance, Sentence 1 (passive) is preferable to Sentence 2 (active):

1. A bomb was found in a locker at the National Airport.
2. Someone found a bomb in a locker at the National Airport.

That is, the bomb is more important than the fact that someone found it.

Passive voice has the effect of diminishing individuals by making the agent of an act less apparent. When it is used in legal writing, it can also help to conceal the appearance of guilt or responsibility of individuals. The following is an example of the use of passive voice with just such an intention. It gives the appearance of lessening the severity of a defendant's criminal act:

> At the time this act was committed, the defendant was recalling her personal experience of sexual abuse as a child. Her devious behavior might be expected, under the circumstances.

If the active voice were used here (e.g., *At the time she committed this act*), it would more forcefully emphasize the defendant's guilt.

Punctuation

Punctuation can be a puzzlement when we are writing. This is often because we write differently than we speak: We can ramble on in oral discourse, never having to worry about commas. When we set thoughts down in writing, however, instinct takes over and we place commas wherever a pause seems appropriate. But there are rules regarding punctuation and they have changed to some degree through technology. That is, informational forms that we have acquired through computers (e.g., e-mail and faxes) have become more and more telegraphic, bringing about the elision or omission of some forms of punctuation. Despite this, certain rules remain constant:

• Use commas to set off parenthetical, explanatory, or appositional (e.g., *John, the senior partner,*) words or phrases. A good way to remember this rule is that if you remove those words or phrases set off in commas, the grammatical structure of the sentence is not destroyed.

> *Example:* The defense attorney, in his effort to protect his client, asked the judge to issue a restraining order.

You can remove *in his effort to protect his client* and the sentence is still a sentence.

• Use commas to set off introductory or qualifying words or phrases, especially to avoid confusion.

> *Example:* Commuters who know what they are talking about complain bitterly over the current state of transportation facilities.

This sentence has two possible meanings, depending on whether you use commas or leave them out. If you place a comma after *commuters* and after *who know what they are talking about,* you are referring to *all* commuters. If you omit commas, you are specifying that group of commuters with special savvy regarding transportation facilities.

- Always use commas when separating dependent or subordinate clauses from main or independent clauses:

Example: Unless it is foreclosed for safety reasons, this contract remains valid.

- Use commas in series or when separating certain adjectives from nouns:

Example: The witness is a hard-working, law-abiding, patriotic citizen.

However, if there are two adjectives modifying a noun, a comma may render a different (sometimes ludicrous) meaning:

Example: He is a high, fidelity fanatic.

Does this mean that he is a devoted husband who drinks?

- Use semicolons to separate sentences or complete thoughts:

Example: The Supreme Court remanded the decision; the Appellate Court judges were disappointed.

Here, a semicolon is used instead of a period, although this sentence could be punctuated either way. Good criteria for deciding whether to choose a period or a semicolon are to vary your usage for stylistic reasons and to decide which format best emphasizes your meaning. Also, when the two ideas are very closely related, the semicolon unifies them and is preferable to the period.

- Use a colon to introduce a list or series in a sentence:

Example: Several states have recently adopted this regulatory provision: Georgia, Louisiana, and Texas.

A colon also indicates that a summary or explanation will follow:

Example: Mary is an excellent attorney: efficient, fair-minded, and erudite.

Dashes may be substituted for colons, which serve the same grammatical purpose. However, dashes should be used with discretion—usually for dramatic effect, as with exclamation points!

Modifiers

The key to writing clear sentences is knowing where to place your modifiers. They should be placed close to the words or phrases they relate to. When they appear in the wrong places, your reader has to pause and try to determine what the sentence means. Consider these examples:

> Much like alcohol and cigarettes, children would obviously be urged to stay away from these drugs.

This sentence has a dangling modifier, which means that the opening clause seems to relate to children. (Are children like alcohol and cigarettes?) We need to move the clause and change the wording to something like this:

> Children would obviously be urged to stay away from these drugs, just as they are urged to stay away from alcohol and cigarettes.

Often, when modifiers appear at the ends of sentences instead of next to the words or phrases they modify, the results can be humorous:

> He disputes the point that drug users only hurt themselves with descriptive examples.

It might read:

> He disputes, with descriptive examples, the point that drug users only hurt themselves.

Then, too, a modifier should make the correct connection with its subject:

> His aim seems to be those who already have taken a position.

What is meant by *those?* This is clearer:

> His aim is to persuade those individuals who have already taken a position.

Intelligibility of Sentences

Your objective in writing is to communicate meaning in the clearest, most accurate style possible. The sections you have just read suggest some of the ways to accomplish this at the sentence level. They can be summarized in these guidelines:

- Vary sentence lengths and styles for easier reading.
- Economize in word usage and phrase formation.
- Use precise, factual language, positioned correctly.
- Reserve figurative language for special, emphatic purposes.
- Punctuate clearly.

As I have just pointed out, and as the legal writing community has proclaimed again and again, such composition should be as clear and simple as possible. However, legal argument, by the very fact that it is *legal* argument, frequently is not simple. When the "plain" word is the true equivalent of the legal term, by all means use it. However, many legal terms and phrases, invented and refined for very specific meanings, just do not have everyday equivalents and must be retained.

Following is a passage from an opinion, clearly not simple, that was much admired by renowned Judge Pierre Leval. Note how a complex litigated situation has been expressed in complex but accurate and unadorned terms. When analyzing this passage, you may find it helpful to imagine a particular action that would entail both large and small risks—such as a false alarm—and then apply the particulars here:

> We see no reason why an actor engaging in conduct which entails a large risk of small damage and a small risk of other and greater damage, of the same general sort, from the same forces, and to the same class of persons, should be relieved of responsibility for the latter simply because the chance of its occurrence, if viewed alone, may not have been large enough to require the exercise of care. By hypothesis, the risk of the lesser harm was sufficient to render his disregard of it actionable; the existence of a less likely additional risk that the very forces against whose action he was required to guard would produce other and greater damage than could have been reasonably anticipated should inculpate him further rather than limit his liability.[3]

This lengthy, painstaking passage—obviously hypotactic in style—is praised by Leval in these words: "Dizzying? Without question. But it was not written to entertain. And there is not a superfluous or inexact word in it."[4] It is hard to imagine packing such density into two sentences. Yet if we parse the sentences and separate the main elements of the argument, we find that Leval's assessment holds (my notations appear in brackets):

> [**Primary Assumption**]
> We [**the Court**] see no reason why an actor [**the defendant**] engaging in conduct which entails [**here, "which *he knew* would entail" is understood; i.e., if a retarded teenager pulled the alarm, he would not be culpable**]
> [**a**] a large risk of small damage and
> [**b**] a small risk of other and greater damage,
> [**1**] of the same general sort,
> [**2**] from the same forces,
> [**3**] and to the same class of persons
> [**1, 2, 3 modify a and b**]
> should be relieved of responsibility for the latter [**i.e., b**] simply because the chance of its occurrence, if viewed alone, [**i.e., does not allow qualifying circumstances**] may not have been large enough to require the exercise of care.
> [**Secondary Assumption**]
> By hypothesis, [**i.e., for the sake of argument**] the risk of the lesser harm [**i.e., a**] [**note here a change in terminology: damage → harm**] was sufficient to render his disregard of it actionable; [**i.e., liable**]
> [**Conclusion**]
> the existence of a less likely additional risk [**i.e., b**] that the very forces against whose action he was required to guard would produce other and greater damage than could have been reasonably anticipated
> [**End Focus**]
> should inculpate him further rather than limit his liability.

This passage is a kind of linguistic shuttle that moves forward in a series of clauses referring back to *a* and *b* and their modifiers *1, 2,* and *3.* The end focus of the passage makes a claim for greater blame when there is great likelihood that a "small risk" is ignored, and the lesser but foreseeable risk of "greater damage" is also ignored.

The Paragraph Level

Just as good sentence organization will help you communicate meaning effectively, good paragraph organization does the same. When readers see a paragraph blocked on a page, they expect it to justify itself with a governing theme or idea. Here are some guidelines for writing and managing paragraphs.

Why Do We Need Paragraphs?

We need paragraphs in order to compartmentalize specific parts of a document for several reasons: to sort out the logical, factual segments of our content material; to achieve a rhetorical purpose; and to create clear divisions for easy reading and comprehension. Think of a paragraph as a triangle in opposite positions:

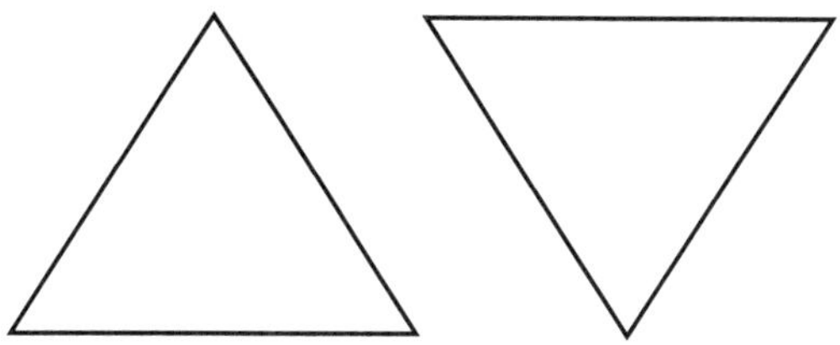

A B

Now, imagine your sentences being placed within the two triangles. In Triangle A, your ideas build as the paragraph progresses, giving the necessary information and increasing your reader's interest and then closing with a summative or completing statement. The reader is ready to move on. In Triangle B, the reverse happens; all the information is packed into the first sentence, while the remainder of the paragraph structure dwindles down to inessentials.

Since our everyday reading matter consists mostly of newspaper articles, we have become accustomed to Style B. A news account delivers the essential points in the first sentence; as the account continues, the information becomes less and less important. How many of us, usually reading hurriedly, finish the account—often continued on some later page of the newspaper?

This form of writing is fair game for journalism, but not for legal writing. Legal writing consists largely of developmental analysis; because it has a different message than journalism, it must also have a different style. Moreover, in journalism, many paragraphs consist of just one sentence, especially at the beginning of a news story. It is easy to internalize this form of reading, since we do not habitually pore through novels or other kinds of prose with such frequency. Thus, it takes some practice to create effective paragraph organization and strategy.

Where Do We Make Paragraphs?

Think of playing a game of checkers or chess. When you move your piece, you pick the direction and square that will best lead you to the finish. The same is true of paragraphing; depending on the context of your argument, you position each paragraph where its inclusion *there* seems inevitable. One way to know you are positioning effectively is to pull a paragraph from its place and insert it randomly somewhere else. If it fits there just as well, then its role in your document is not very important. The same is true of a block or series of paragraphs, which you might pull and move to another place. Does this block or series belong together and in the place you have designated for it?

In order to ensure good paragraph positioning, keep these two criteria in mind:

1. Readers expect you to organize the material for them; this leaves them free to absorb your ideas without delay or confusion.
2. Much of legal writing requires logical order of ideas, exactitude of analysis, and overall internal cohesion. One way to know that your paragraphs are in the right place is to make an outline of the contents you will include in your paper. Then practice moving topic areas around until they have the best strategic sequence. (Refer to Chapter 1 for a discussion of outlines.)

How Do We Make Paragraphs?

You probably have stored somewhere in your memory the notion that a paragraph must begin with a topic or thesis sentence. Then, in your reading, you may have discovered essays—by good stylists—in which such creatures do not appear. They need not. A topic sentence is useful when you need to signal the subject for your paragraph, but there are other ways to introduce both a single paragraph and a block of paragraphs for a section of your text. Here are some tactics for beginning a paragraph; they might be called the Golden Dozen Openers:

- Tell an anecdote.
- Anticipate reader rejection of what will follow and offer reassurance.
- Refer to some dramatic statistics.
- Ask a controversial question.
- Try the shock technique of a provocative statement.
- Relate your topic to a current event or controversy.
- Give helpful background information.
- Use a quotation from literature or from an authority.
- Narrow the focus from the general to the specific.
- Refer to a historical event.
- Make a striking contrast.
- Use a witty passage that incorporates wordplay or a pun.

Some of these may actually turn out to *be* your topic or thesis sentences, but if you think of them as attention grabbers, you will be more daring. The same holds true for writing the conclusions of paragraphs or paragraph blocks. Unless it really serves your rhetorical intentions, do not make your conclusion a trite repetition of what you have already said. Trust, don't bore, your reader. And be sure that the final sentence of your paragraph delivers a transition to what will follow. No paragraph is an island unto itself.

What Are the Kinds of Paragraphs?

You have the choice of paragraph length. As mentioned earlier regarding style in general, interesting legal writing is varied. Intersperse long paragraphs with short ones; their content should determine which to select. In either case, be sure that the internal parts are linked. That is, do not rename ideas or issues in order to avoid redundancy (this may confuse the reader) and do not refer to an idea discussed early in the paragraph by calling it "it" later on (several ideas may have interceded in between). Although redundancy can be annoying to the reader, at times it is necessary in order to avoid confusion.

The Complete Text Level

If you have written your sentences and paragraphs according to the stylistic recommendations we have discussed, chances are that your complete text will be effective. Here are some other factors to consider in overall construction.

Theme

Often in a trial, a skilled attorney will structure the arguments for a case with a theme that he or she injects intermittently or repeats at crucial points. The theme could be a statement, a phrase, or just a word that unifies the information and justifies the attorney's position. This applies to many types of legal prose besides trial proceedings (exceptions are certain formatted documents such as codes, regulatory procedures, and contracts).

Themes are especially useful when you are advocating a cause or prompting your audience to action. For example, if you are writing to a zoning committee, arguing that a proposed high-tech building development will destroy parks and recreational facilities much needed in a low-income area, a theme such as *Kids come before computers* may strengthen your case. Also, when a theme stresses worthwhile goals such as fair treatment, individual responsibility, and civic pride, the universal appeal that it carries will strengthen your factual content.

Tone

Tone is the voice or personality that you convey in all writing, whether it is a personal letter or a professional memorandum. Tone surfaces in every aspect of the composition process: choice of diction, opening and closing remarks, placement of facts, and even punctuation.

What you want to achieve through tone is a rapport with your reader. Here is an example. At some point in your school life, you were likely given this assignment when you returned to classes in the fall: Write an essay on How I Spent My Summer. If your reaction was "Oh, no, what do I tell this teacher?" the chances are that the tone of your essay was stiffly formal and impersonal—and not terribly good. But if you wrote the essay as a letter to a close friend, eager to share your summer experiences, the chances are that your tone was more effective and communicative.

In legal writing, which often requires communicating with resistant, sometimes contentious, audiences, tone is especially important. Like walking a tightrope, you must find a balance between sounding self-righteous and self-effacing, between sounding arrogant and unduly humble. Also, it means keeping your voice consistent. That is, if you switch from sarcasm in one paragraph to congenial discourse in the next paragraph, your reader may have some cause for distrust, confusion, or skepticism. Finally, the best tone in legal writing displays integrity and open-mindedness on the part of a writer. When this is present, even a fierce adversary may find your position deserving of reflection.

Loaded Language

Loaded language is generally associated with those genres that appeal more to emotive responses than to cognitive responses (i.e., editorials, advertisements, and political campaign speeches). Loaded language does not fare well in legal writing. Rather, load your writing with rational, logical, and factual statements, which, with careful analysis and exactitude, will deliver a more powerful message. Although you may deplore certain principles or actions discussed in the subject you are writing about, do not make this evident through your language. Avoid coloring or slanting statements with derogatory or suggestive adjectives or descriptions. President Ronald Reagan may have felt free to dub Russia "the evil empire," but such license is unsuitable in legal writing.

Style and Gender

There has been rapid and widespread change in writing to eliminate sexist language. Many women are offended by the sexist use of language and regard gender-neutral writing as a way to correct this. The challenge is to get rid of male pronouns (*he, his,* and *him*) in contexts where females are intended to be included. Sometimes this cannot be accomplished without some loss of elegance, but there are ways of dealing with the problem in less awkward ways. Here are some techniques for avoiding sexist language without sacrificing clarity and precision:

- Use sex-neutral terms—for example, *workers* rather than *workmen.*
- Omit the pronoun—for example:

  On reaching the age of 75, a director must resign office.
- Avoid *man* words—for example, *the average person* rather *than the average man; humanity* or *people* rather than *mankind* or *man; workforce* rather than *manpower.*
- Use the plural instead of the singular—for example:

  All the jurors took their role seriously.

  rather than

  Each juror took his role seriously.
- Recast sentences by using a participle—for example:

  A person must give 7 days' notice before lodging an appeal.

  rather than

  A person must give 7 days' notice before he lodges an appeal.

Although certain modifications in writing gender-neutral language may seem stilted, such as *waitperson* for *waitress,* it is more important that we take care to avoid stereotypes that are fast becoming obsolete.

Avoiding Stereotypes

Since so much of legal writing is shared with the public, or is at least accessible in the public domain, individuals and groups of individuals must be described in that writing accurately and without bias. Anything that appeals to clichés or stereotypes regarding various segments of the population must be avoided. For example, making an allusion about urban populations may be taken as an indirect criticism of ethnic groups that might live in urban areas. At best, such allusions are regarded as arrogant or elitist; at worst, they are considered biased or prejudiced.

Examples of Style

Here are some writing excerpts you can test for their stylistic effectiveness—or lack thereof:

EXAMPLE 3.1 Transfer Policy Statement

This passage, from the 1985–86 University of Maryland *Undergraduate Catalog,* is a description of the state of Maryland's higher-education transfer policies. Since many state residents (over 50 percent) spend their first two college-level years at a community college and then transfer to a four-year institution in the system, a document explaining transfer policies is of great importance to them. Students frequently complained that the policies, as put forth in this passage, were unclear and needed revision:

> The intended principal benefactor is the student, who is best served by current information about programs and protected by firm arrangements among the public segments of higher education in Maryland which permit him to plan a total degree program from the outset. With successful academic performance, he or she can make uninterrupted progress even though transfer is involved. The measure of the effectiveness of the plan is maximum transferability of college level credits within the parameters of this agreement. Essentially, transfer and native students are to be governed by the same academic rules and regulations.
>
> In a complementary way the State's interests are served by having its higher education resources used optimally by reducing the time taken to complete a degree through the avoidance of repeated class experience.
>
> The institutional interests are protected also by the systematic approach; institutions are relieved of the uncertainties of unplanned articulation without becoming production line enterprises.

How and why is this passage faulty? First, it is written in a style most students find unclear (e.g., *uncertainties of unplanned articulation*). Second, it is vague in explaining what the students want to know about transfer policies. Third, it brings in *the State's interests* and the *institutional interests,* matters that transfer students find extraneous to the information they need at the moment. The gist of the document might be appropriate for a University Board of Trustees report but it fails as a guide for students.

EXAMPLE 3.2 **Conclusion from Paper on Legalizing Physician-Assisted Suicide**

The second example is a concluding paragraph from a student paper that argues for legalization of physician-assisted suicide. As you read it, think of how it could be stylistically improved:

> To avoid the slippery slope and to validate the position of the state, which is to protect life, legalized assisted suicide would have to be subject to regulations. These regulations would have to restrict such practices to adults who are terminally ill and mentally competent. However, it would be preferable to minimize the red tape. The appropriate objective would be to ensure competence, a terminal diagnosis, and the lack of possibility of recovery, and to prescribe the proper drugs that would allow the patients, in the privacy of their own homes, to decide when they can stand the suffering no longer.

Although concrete recommendations are made here, the paragraph lacks organization, fragmenting into disconnected ideas. The sentence *However, it would be preferable to minimize the red tape* needs a transition to link it with the preceding sentence. It also needs a transition to the one that follows. As this sentence is written, the reader expects to learn *how* to minimize the red tape. Also, the sentence beginning *The appropriate objective . . .* mixes phrases and clauses randomly, including an unclear verb phrase (*ensure competence*) that is not grammatically parallel to the remaining verb phrases. The sentence shifts from lack of detail (*a terminal diagnosis*) to too much detail (*to prescribe the proper drugs that would allow the patients, in the privacy of their own homes, to decide when they can stand the suffering no longer*).

EXAMPLE 3.3 Introduction to Paper on High-Speed Police Chases

This sample, also written by a student, is the opening paragraph for a paper that argues against police high-speed chases in pursuit of nonviolent criminals. Evaluate its stylistic elements and decide whether it makes an effective introduction:

> It begins with a simple traffic stop or arrest attempt which soon evolves into a deadly, high-speed chase. An offender, desperately trying to avoid arrest, leads police officers through a labyrinth of streets, alleys, and byways. Sometimes at speeds of only 10 mph, sometimes at speeds in excess of 100 mph, pursuits like this will end up on the wrong side of the street, over sidewalks, and through playgrounds—often with tragic results. For Maryland's most reprehensible offenders, police pursuits are an unavoidable aspect of law enforcement. However, what is troubling is that some deadly chases are after low-level, misdemeanor offenders. These "trivial pursuits" are wrong for several reasons: They jeopardize the safety of citizens and police staff; they are costly; and they create legal dilemmas in which the state is held accountable for damages as well as injuries or fatalities of innocent people. Some police agencies have begun restricting their officers from engaging in such pursuits. I intend to argue that other agencies, statewide, should follow suit.

I think you will agree that this paragraph draws your attention. It opens with a hypothetical anecdote about a police chase, but it quickly converts the anecdote into an actual problem that we must confront. The paragraph concludes by stating the purpose of the paper—to advocate statewide restriction of this practice when it applies to nonviolent offenders. Stylistically, the simple diction (spiced with wordplay in *trivial pursuits*), the orderly transition of ideas from sentence to sentence, and the closing purpose statement combine into a well-organized introduction.

EXAMPLE 3.4 Excerpts from Court Decisions on Voting District Boundaries

Here are excerpts from two U.S. Supreme Court Justices' opinions on a Court decision. The decision, delivered on June 29, 1995, concerns district boundaries and whether the consideration of race to increase African American voter power in an electoral district is unconstitutional. Justice Anthony Kennedy wrote the majority opinion; Justice Ruth Bader Ginsburg wrote the dissent. Analyze the two excerpts, equally eloquent in their own way, applying the stylistic principles developed in this chapter.

From Justice Kennedy's Opinion

The plaintiff's burden is to show, either through circumstantial evidence of a district's shape and demographics or more direct evidence going to legislative purpose, that race was the predominant factor motivating the legislature's decision to place a significant number of voters within or without a particular district.

To make this showing, a plaintiff must prove that the legislature subordinated traditional race-neutral districting principles, including but not limited to compactness, contiguity, respect for political divisions or communities defined by actual shared interests, to racial considerations.

From Justice Ginsburg's Opinion

Legislative districting is highly political business. When race is the issue, however, we have recognized the need for judicial intervention to prevent dilution of minority voting strength. Generations of rank discrimination against African Americans, as citizens and voters, account for that surveillance. Apportionment schemes, by their very nature, assemble people in groups. That ethnicity defines some of these groups is a political reality. Until now, no constitutional infirmity has been seen in districting Irish or Italian voters together, for example.

Justice Kennedy's style is clearly hypotactic. The sentences are lengthy, amplified by subordinate clauses. In the first sentence, the main thought (*The plaintiff's burden is to show*) is not completed until the end (*that race was the predominant factor*). The delayed verb is qualified by details in the intervening subordinate clause (*either through circumstantial evidence of a district's shape and demographics or more direct evidence going to legislative purpose*). Two kinds of evidence are required: circumstantial and more direct. The second sentence begins with a dependent clause (*To make this showing*), followed by an independent clause (*a plaintiff must prove that the legislature subordinated traditional race-neutral districting principles . . . to racial considerations*). As you can see, this clause is interrupted by a modifier that supplements the information (*including but not limited to compactness, contiguity, respect for political subdivisions*).

This excerpt also contains a number of abstract nouns and noun phrases (e.g., *contiguity* and *legislative purpose*). Put together, the hypotactic sentence usage, combined with the abstract (as opposed to concrete) word usage, produces a distinctly formal style. Justice Kennedy's style can be seen as deliberately underscoring the kinds of legal evidence required for making a Supreme Court decision.

Justice Ginsburg's style, on the other hand, is active and businesslike, pointing quickly to the actions to be taken and the persons affected. Her sentences as well as her subordinate clauses are direct and relatively short (*Legislative districting is highly political business* and *as citizens and voters*). Moreover, her choice of diction comes near to everyday discourse, insofar as she brings representative examples into her writing (*no constitutional infirmity has been seen in districting Irish or Italian voters together*).

Kennedy and Ginsburg each projects a tone, or voice, that bespeaks a genuine belief in what he or she is writing. There is no better way to summarize what is meant by that slippery word, *style.*

EXERCISES

3.1 *Sentences to Correct*

Correct the errors in grammar and punctuation in these sentences:

1. After we eat John will do the dishes.
2. Two ships in the American fleet is not accounted for.
3. Gee, I could of had a V-8!

4. I found a dollar walking home.
5. The passive voice is to be avoided.
6. Last but not least, avoid clichés like the plague. They're old hat.
7. Never use a long word when a diminutive one will do.
8. Take the bull by the hand and avoid mixing metaphors.
9. Many panes in the window was broken and dirty.
10. If you reread your work, you can find on rereading a great deal of repetition can be avoided by rereading and editing.

3.2 *Punctuation*

Insert all necessary punctuation in the following paragraph. Do not change the beginnings or ends of any sentences.

> Management then may establish a favorable environment and sound procedures for good report writing on the other hand it may unknowingly cause poor report writing. One irate division manager showed us a report which could only be called a monstrosity. It was three inches thick. It had no table of contents no appendixes no summary nothing to help the manager find his way through it. In order to get anything out of it he would have to read the whole report an eight- or ten-hour job. When we talked with him he was going to fire the writer of the report.

3.3 *Rewriting Legal Language*

Make the following passage more precise by reducing it to the most necessary information.

> The above-entitled matter came on for hearing before the undersigned on November 5, pursuant to a motion and notice thereof, duly served and filed, in which the motion petitioner moved the court for an order (1) dismissing the complaint herein or (2) in the alternative, for an order remanding the said matter to the hearing examiner for the presentation of such additional evidence as may be necessary.
>
> The parties were not present but were represented by counsel, John D. Lewis for the petitioner and Prudence O.

Jackson, special assistant attorney general, for respondent. The motion was based upon the affidavit of John D. Lewis and upon all the files, records and proceedings. Both parties submitted memoranda in support of their respective positions.

Upon all the files, records and proceedings had and filed in said matter, arguments and memoranda of Counsel and after due consideration of the same, it is ordered (1) that petitioner's motion to dismiss the complaint herein be and the same is denied.

3.4 *Using Gender-Neutral Language*

Rewrite the following sentences to eliminate sexist language.

1. How many people will we need to man this investigation?
2. Prosecutors often neglect their wives and children.
3. Man's greatest achievement was the development of his ability to speak.
4. The opinions of the man on the street often show racial prejudice.
5. Of the 300 students admitted to the law school, half were coeds.

3.5 *Noninflammatory Writing*

The following paragraph is an illustration of inflammatory writing. Improve it according to these instructions:

- Indicate what words you would change in the paragraph.
- Substitute words or phrases that convey the meaning effectively, but without introducing strong connotations.

A judge may well cringe with horror at the thought that the defendant, Jay Monroe, was responsible for the children who attend his Monroe Day Care Center. No reasonable jury would believe that his refusal to allow parents to visit unannounced is anything but a back alley tactic to conceal filthy, obscene activity. To let this reprehensible man go free is to jeopardize those innocent babes who would fall into his trap.

3.6 *Examining a Legal Quotation*

Look for a passage in a news article or magazine article that quotes a lawyer or judge on a current issue. Evaluate the quotation for its stylistic dimensions. Try to employ as many of the style criteria discussed in this chapter as you can.

ENDNOTES

1. Todd Purdum, "Intern's Counsel Coached Peers on Art of Deposition," *New York Times,* January 25, 1998, p. NE 13.
2. *Schoellhammer's Hatboro Manor Inc. v. Local Joint Executive Board of Philadelphia,* 231 A2d 160 (1967).
3. Pierre Leval, "Judicial Opinion as Literature," *Law's Stories: Narrative and Rhetoric in the Law* (New Haven. CT: Yale University Press, 1996).
4. Ibid.

4

Narrative in Legal Prose

When you glanced at the title of this chapter, did you question its appropriateness in a textbook about legal writing? After all, aren't narratives just stories—works that one reads for pleasure in literature courses? The answer is yes, legal narrative uses many of the same devices and strategies found in literary works. However, legal narrative is not written merely for aesthetic purposes, but also to produce evidence, to resolve issues, to record information in a coherent account and—if these purposes are satisfied—to persuade.

Perhaps you can best understand what legal narrative is by looking at these three narratives, which, although extremely brief, are narratives nonetheless:

Example 1: The king died and the queen died.

Example 2: The king died, and then the queen died.

Example 3: The king died, and then the queen died of grief.

These examples introduce you to two essential narrative elements: time and cause. Look at the changes that occur in these examples, depending on the presence or absence of these elements:

- Example 1 relates two independent events: The king died and the queen died. Neither the time nor the cause is stated.
- Example 2 introduces the important element of time in narrative: First the king died, and *then* the queen died.
- Example 3 introduces the important element of cause in narrative: The queen died *because* the king died.

An aspect of narrative coherence that is especially relevant to legal prose can be observed by the fact that my explanation of Example 3 added something—the word *because*—which was not in the example. This underscores the particular force of time and cause as narrative elements. We *assume,* on the basis of an inherent "story sense," that an event that follows another event in the narrative chain may have been *caused by* the previous event.

However, in our mental search for a causal connection, logic also plays a part. While grief over a preceding death may well have been a cause for the queen's death, the situation would change radically if Example 3 had read *The king died, and then the queen died of food poisoning.* Therefore, as you construct an account of the events of your case or argument, you must remain aware of the effect your audience's inherent desire for narrative coherence will have on their determination of guilt or innocence, right or wrong, or that which is allowable or prohibited.

Having demonstrated in the three examples just discussed the three essential concepts of legal narrative as event, time, and cause, I now move on to develop the particular goals of this chapter:

- To demonstrate how inseparable narrative is from all forms of legal writing
- To discuss the different devices used for writing legal narrative
- To illustrate the structures found in legal narrative

Forms of Narrative and Legal Issues

If you are working in a law firm, your client will frequently be in the position of the accuser or the accused in such cases as breach of contract, robbery, domestic dispute, harassment in the workplace, environmental violation, diplomatic immunity—the list seems endless. For each of these possibilities, you must first find out *what happened.* Next, on the basis of this knowledge, you then help your client put together an account of the facts in an accurate and coherent manner. This account will better succeed if it demonstrates narrative skill. Bernard Jackson, a noted legal scholar, strongly underscores this: "A simple short, true story might not be believed, while a complex, false story might be overwhelmingly believed if it exhibited greater structural coherence."[1]

EXAMPLE 4.1 Diplomatic Immunity

My first illustration of the use of legal narrative is taken from a student position statement. It is an introduction for a longer paper on violations that have resulted from the privileges of diplomatic immunity:

> On November 29, 1982, Antonia Da Silveira, Jr., the 23-year-old son of the then Brazilian Ambassador to the United States, shot an American bouncer several times outside a Washington, DC, nightclub, after getting into an argument with him. Da Silveira was detained by local authorities until his identity was revealed; then, at the request of State Department officials, he was released with all charges against him dropped. The young man immediately departed from the United States, and his father was subsequently released of his duties the following year. While this story may be shocking to most Americans, it is not an uncommon occurrence in the practice of international law. The Brazilian family, with approval from their government, chose to exercise their rights and privileges under diplomatic immunity.

As you can see, the facts of this event are delivered in narrative form, an effective way to quickly gain the reader's attention and emotional concern. Next, the student grounds this narrative by providing a legal definition of *diplomatic immunity* (see Chapter 2 for discussion of *legal definitions*). This clarifies the basis for the actions that explain the Da Silveira story:

> Diplomatic immunity under Article 29 of the Vienna Convention states that "the person of a diplomatic agent shall be inviolable. He shall not be liable to any form of arrest or detention. The receiving State shall treat him with due respect and shall take all steps to prevent attack on his person, freedom, or dignity."

The text that follows this definition returns to the narrative mode for a brief background of diplomatic immunity:

> The application of this definition of diplomatic immunity dates back to ancient times. Primitive societies developed methods of conducting wars, negotiating peace, and discussing trade issues. Most often, these transactions involved sending messengers to conduct some aspect of business. The receiving community recognized the free movement of these messengers and their immunity from local laws. Thus began the concept of "diplomatic immunity," which evolved to the establishment of resident diplomats and ambassadors.

Since the student's paper emphasizes the contemporary paradoxes—and violations—resulting from such privileges accorded to diplomats, further details of the 1961 Vienna Convention on Diplomatic Relations, signed into treaty, are offered:

> The Treaty listed all the immunities and privileges under several categories. These included delineating the purpose of immunities; ensuring the protection of premises (i.e., the buildings in which official business is conducted as well as the diplomat's residence); and making secure the diplomat's person, records, and communications. Moreover, not only are diplomatic agents exempt from criminal civil jurisdiction of the receiving state, but the exemptions are valid for the diplomat's family as well.

The student, careful to remain objective, next discusses the ways in which *both* visiting diplomats and their host states sometimes equally abuse and disregard the objectives underlying Article 29:

> In recent years, many questions have been raised regarding the application of diplomatic immunity under Article 29 of the Vienna Convention. More specifically, it is the criminal activity of certain diplomats that ignites controversy. As is evident from the Da Salveira case, an increasing number of diplomats and their families feel they are above the law. A drunk driving incident in

which a Georgian diplomat killed a young girl in Washington, DC, is a more recent example (1997) of such disregard. This is evident even in minor transgressions, such as the proliferation of parking tickets, for which diplomats are not penalized.

It is equally important to note that most diplomats do not break the law and are in need of protection, especially during this era of burgeoning civil wars and ethnic strife. The hostage crisis in Tehran in 1981, which involved American diplomatic personnel, is an example. The American hostages were held by the host country for 444 days until the United States appealed to the World Court and, by the terms of the Vienna Convention, received an order for their release. In this crisis, the host country, Iran, was guilty of blatant disregard for diplomatic immunity.

These passages from the position paper are acceptable to us as readers because we naturally structure any occurrence in an anecdotal or storylike manner. This is the case in all levels of legal writing. Storytelling in the law is closer to such genres as journalism and history than it is to literary works, since a dominant purpose in journalism and history is, like the law, to record facts and events. In fact, the narrative status of law's methodology (i.e., its shaping choices of language), its detail and order, is difficult to even recognize as a separable technique. The law itself implies a *dependence* on the role of narrative in its methodology. Storytelling has always been a seminal or organic aspect, but it plays an even greater role today. As a writer, you need to be aware of its increased significance. Some reasons for the growing importance of storytelling are discussed next.

Political and social groups are currently demanding that their arguments be framed in narrative patterns. This is in opposition to the more traditional, abstract modes of legal argument. These groups place an emphasis on narrative for culturally recurrent issues such as race and feminist legal theory. Minorities, women, and diverse marginal groups contend that "legalese" perpetuates the existing power structure. Since the narrative model of writing belongs to a popular level of social knowledge, it is preferred over an abstract legal style, which is considered elitist and specialized. For example, abstract legal writing uses terms understood through reason or logic (e.g., behavior is characterized as *prohibited* or *requisite*). A more narrativized approach would characterize behavior with such words as *good* or *bad* or *virtuous* or *evil.* These words evoke in us a more compelling, human response.

What is the significance of this demand for more narrative to you as a writer? The answer is that though you must not use narrative to subvert the rationality or justice of the law, you should appreciate its potential for persuasion, while using it both ethically and with discretion. Put more legalistically, narrative should serve to promote the following objectives:

- To reduce hostility between any disputants
- To command a sense of control in a dispute or argument
- To gain acceptance of the outcomes of such disputes or arguments

With regard to the frequent presence of narrative in legal writing, it is fair to say that it pervades every aspect of the legal system. Narrative appears in routine contract settlements, common pretrial pleadings, and even in lofty legal and historical decisions handed down by the Supreme Court.

EXAMPLE 4.2 Opinion by Justice John Paul Stevens

Here is an illustration of the use of narrative in a Supreme Court opinion, delivered on May 27, 1997, which held that a sitting president is not immune from litigation while in office. This excerpt, which is rather graphic in spots, contains details abut the alleged behavior of President William Clinton in a hotel room. To those who are familiar with the content and details of Supreme Court decisions, the inclusion of passages such as these indicates the change taking place in legal prose. Here is the excerpt:

> [Jones's] allegations principally describe events that are said to have occurred on the afternoon of May 8, 1991, during an official conference held at the Excelsior Hotel in Little Rock, Arkansas. The Governor delivered a speech at the conference; respondent, i.e., *Paula Corbin Jones*, working as a state employee, staffed the registration desk. She alleges that [Arkansas State Trooper Danny] Ferguson persuaded her to leave her desk and to visit the Governor in a business suite at the hotel, where he made "abhorrent" sexual advances that she vehemently rejected. She further claims that her superiors at work subsequently dealt with her in a hostile and rude manner, and changed her duties to

> punish her for rejecting those advances. Finally, she alleges that after petitioner was elected President, Ferguson defamed her by making a statement to a reporter that implied she had accepted petitioner's alleged overtures, and that various persons authorized to speak for the President branded her a liar by denying that the incident had occurred.[2]

It is clear that this passage is built not only on fact but on a *reported* account, which has the flavor of fiction. However, the remainder of Justice Stevens's opinion contains elements not present in fictional stories—namely, the citation of other cases. Therefore, Justice Stevens brings in precedents to justify Jones's right to trial while President Clinton is still in office. Stevens's purpose in doing this is to dispel the fear that allowing this trial to take place will prompt numerous other litigants to bring charges against a president while serving office:

> In the more than 200-year history of the Republic, only three sitting Presidents have been subject to suits for their private actions. If the past is any indicator, it seems unlikely that a deluge of such litigation will ever engulf the Presidency. Complaints against Theodore Roosevelt and Harry Truman had been dismissed before they took office. . . . Two companion cases arising out of an automobile accident were filed against John F. Kennedy in 1960 during the Presidential campaign. After taking office, he unsuccessfully argued that his status as Commander in Chief gave him a right to a stay. . . . [See the Glossary for a definition of *stay.*] The matter was settled out of court. Thus, none of those cases sheds any light on the constitutional issue before us.[3]

Clearly, even this passage, which invokes several legal precedents, resorts to some use of narrative. But the inclusion of Stevens's restatement of the "hotel" episode, whether fact or fiction, would not be as effective without its situational detail, which appeals to the reader's imagination. The passage also illustrates how, in legal writing, fact and fiction can become bedfellows (forgive the pun).

Thus, two distinct genres—literary narrative and legal discourse—are joined. The Jones/Clinton narrative is heightened in part by minority rights advocates' avowal of storytelling as protection against what is considered a male-dominated legal system. In this instance, the advocates are making a feminist outcry against sexual harassment. It is a narrative whose sources embed a metaphoric theme. Depending on one's interpretation, its theme could be one or several of the following: exploitation, lust, greed, and power. These are also the key themes on which the story has been built. Given its selection of details, ordered meanings were created. As a *legal* story, it contains chronology and causation, leading to our next inquiry regarding legal narrative: the different devices for writing legal narrative.

Devices for Writing Legal Narrative

You have seen how the law is not strictly constructed on fact alone but on some form of discourse that necessarily includes story. We will now examine those devices of story that underlie legal writing.

Plot

Narrative in legal writing often appears in the form of a case scenario, the details of which ultimately become known as the proposed or disputed evidence for a case. Both the defense and prosecution will do the following: present evidence that will contradict the other side's evidence; introduce questions regarding the opposition's credibility; and rely on what its side considers a standard of justice. This is configured into what we all recognize as the *plot* in which a story is embedded. It is a device so familiar to us that we take its meaning for granted. For the present purposes, however, here is a working definition of *plot* that is applicable to legal narrative:

> *Plot* is an artificial rather than a natural ordering of events. Its function is to simplify life by imposing order thereon. It would be possible, though most tedious, to recite *all* incidents, *all* events passing through the minds of one or more characters during a period of, say, a week. The demands of *plot* stipulate that the author *select* from this welter of events and reflection those items that have a certain *unity*, that point to a certain end, and have a common relation represent not more than two or three threads of interest and activity. *Plot* brings order out of life. . . . In this sense it focuses and clarifies life.[4]

As a legal writer, you become the author whose task is stated in this definition. You select those items to achieve a certain *unity*, one that best supports your position.

EXAMPLE 4.3 The Case of *Alabama v. Mary Smith*

The following trial narrative delivers details of a case in plot form. As you read it, look for those incidents and events that may or may not give it unity:

> In the spring of 1995, Mary Smith shot her father, Frank Smith, numerous times in the head and chest, killing him. Mary, a teenager of sixteen, then called the police and reported her actions. Mary's parents had been separated and the separation agreement stipulated that Frank return once a week to visit his daughter at her home.
>
> Mary testified that she shot her father when he came to her house, on February 1, 1995, to keep him from "hurting me anymore." She also alleged that her father had started sexually abusing her when she was fourteen, fondling her breasts and climbing on top of her. However, she also said in that two-year period he would telephone her to meet with him at an apartment which he owned as a real estate developer. The first time they met in the apartment, he raped her and the rape episodes continued thereafter in the apartment.
>
> The prosecutor challenged Mary's credibility because she had not reported the repeated rapes, only the fondling scenes that happened in her house, when she first talked to police. This was later revealed. Moreover, no one had ever seen her go into the apartment with her father. The district attorney also argued that this was premeditated murder, since it happened at her house and she had planned to be alone with her father in the house. This claim, by the district attorney, derived from the fact that Mary had sent her mother out on an errand the day of his expected visit, saying "I can handle Daddy."
>
> In her own defense, Mary maintained that she had never told anyone about the rapes, not even her mother, because her father had threatened to burn down the house if she did. It was only after repeated interrogation that Mary revealed the rapes. Mary's mother, testifying in defense of her daughter, said that she had once seen her husband fondling her daughter when she was "little," and that after that episode she had watched her husband "like a hawk."[5]

Pretend that you are a juror—and thus a fact finder in the case—who would have to decide whether Mary's story is true. That is, does it justify the murder of her father? This would require you as a juror to believe that Mary was in imminent danger of death or forcible rape at the time she committed the murder.

The judgment regarding this case is mainly based on evidence produced by a plot. Does the story have unity? Does it ring true, or does the rape admission sound like a fabrication to justify the murder?

Assumptions Regarding Audience

In the process of writing legal narrative, it is important to keep in mind the *assumptions* that will be made by your audience, legal colleagues, prospective jurors, and anyone else who plays a role in legal judgment. There are various levels of assumption and background ideas that you may or may not share with your audience. If we take the preceding narrative on Mary Smith as an example, there are gaps in the account that must be filled. Any responsible reader of this narrative would avoid a frivolous or unreasonable interpretation and attempt to confront the overtones that are embedded in it. As a story, it effectively aims at certain values and standards of human behavior. Since there were no witnesses to the murder, or to the events leading up to the murder, the reader makes assumptions about the story by using the same criteria used for any other narrative. The following are criteria to keep in mind:

- *Revealing detail:* Select those words or phrases that give the most accurate account of a narrative.
- *Implication:* Determine how a narrative puts a point across without actually providing factual information.
- *Prevailing characteristics:* Select that part of a narrative that complies with your expectations regarding human behavior and actions.
- *Presumptive evidence:* Select that part of a narrative that may be alibi testimony. (See the Glossary for definition of *presumptive evidence.*)

Description

Any narrative in legal writing will contain descriptive passages. Not only do narrative descriptions establish the presumed authenticity of an account but they also link chronology, filling in the particulars of what happens, how it happens, and to whom it happens. Description is the ordering connector of each "and then" . . . "and then" in a story. However, in legal writing there are lines of argument that must be factored into description. The following are several ways in which lines of argument act as devices for narrative description:

- Use a characterization as a way to interpret an action.

  Example: Depending on whether you are participating in the defense or the prosecution in a case about car theft by a teenager, your description will characterize the same act differently (e.g., the teenager is either "just a kid who foolishly took a joy ride" or a "felonious offender bent on criminal action").

- Compare public interest, or that which is best for society as a whole, with private feelings.

  Example: In a debate that pits the use of animals for medical research against animal rights, how do you describe the process whereby monkeys' brains are dissected?

- Use correlatives or reciprocal processes/relationships.

  Example: Describe the burdens made on a homeless mother of five when hotels serving as temporary residences are prohibited from functioning as such by city officials. Then describe the negative effect that using hotels for this purpose would have on tourism, as related by a Chamber of Commerce executive.

- Emphasize how unbelievable or unlikely an event is.

  Example: If you were the prosecutor in the murder trial summarized on page 83, describe the ways in which Mary Smith's account is very hard to accept.

Perspective

As you have seen, narrative in legal writing arouses interest and curiosity. In the classical world, people argued their own cases in the courts of law, defending themselves and their ideas before the assembly. They called these arguments *narratio,* which for ancient rhetoricians was that part of the oration that presented the facts of the case. Moreover, it was believed that *narratio* could not be separated from description—that essential component to arouse interest and curiosity.

Ancient rhetoricians also believed that there were several ways to narrate an event, given the perspective. In literary terms, this refers to *point of view.* Transfer this notion of perspective to the present day and consider how a political demonstration would be described from the perspective of the demonstrators, the police, the public onlookers, or the newscaster describing it on television. Each would bring a different perspective (sometimes called *angle* or *slant*) to the story, inventing it according to such criteria as the following:

- The dynamism of this event and its potential to bring about change
- The ideological purpose for this event, which is to disrupt or perpetuate a sociocultural practice, pattern, or system
- The isolated nature of this event, which is regarded as bizarre or even perverse

Structure in Legal Narrative

In everyday conversation, we produce narratives on every topic imaginable. We have numerous options when structuring these conversations, from changing the subject, to linking unrelated topics, to withholding details, to digressing, and so on. Legal narrative is not quite as open ended. Depending on the audience that receives the narrative (e.g., client/lawyer, lawyer/lawyer, lawyer/jury), certain procedures determine what is allowable and what is not.

In a sense, then, basic narratives are controlled and organized differently under the law. There are rules of exclusion that prohibit certain kinds of speech, prohibit certain subjects, and even prohibit certain kinds of discourse to take place. For example, witnesses in any type of litigation are limited to telling stories according to a rule-ordered, question/answer structure. Hearsay narratives are often considered inadmissible (although there are exceptions), as are speculative narratives about how situations or events appeared to witnesses.

Depending on the context in which your narrative will be positioned, you should comply with specific structures. However, despite the context, our objective must always be to observe ethical standards. People's differences must be respected. There is no justification for bias or prejudice toward individuals or groups because of their sex, race, religion, or ethnic origin.

EXAMPLE 4.4 A Domestic Dispute

Let us take, for example, the photo in Figure 4.1, which was published in a special edition of *Life* magazine (October 1996). It captures a moment in a real-life event that was explained in the *Life* issue. However, this explanation has been deleted so that you can structure your own narrative for it. Here are some instructions for writing the narrative:

- Suppose that you are asked to write an official report (e.g., as a parole officer) on the details of this photo for a forthcoming hearing.
- Give an explanatory, factually appropriate title to the photo (nothing cute or clever like "All in the Family" or "Loveboat").

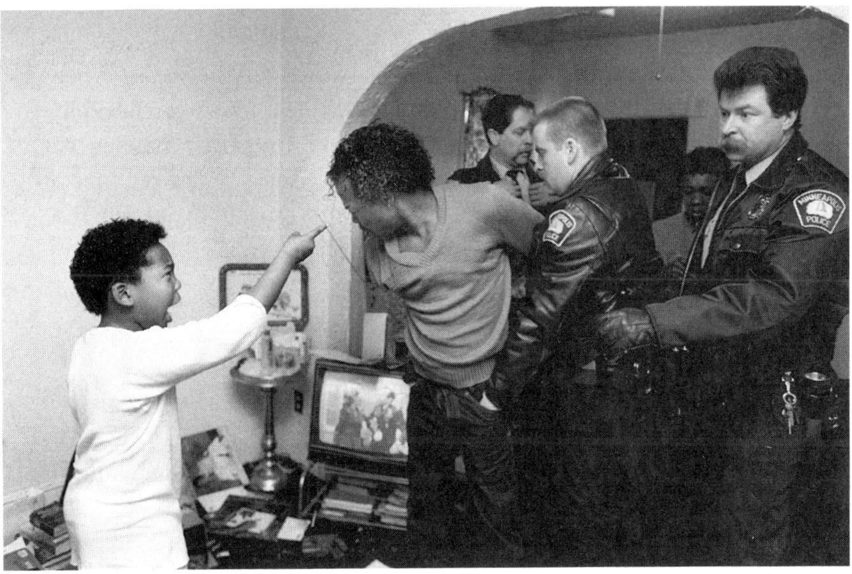

FIGURE 4.1 Photo for Composing Narrative

Source: Reprinted with permission from Domestic Abuse Awareness, Inc.

- Tell the story objectively, using the third-person linguistic form. Interpret the visual clues you see in the photo, but do not add suppositions for which you have no evidence.
- Do not editorialize.
- Consider the photo as a sort of "still" from a movie and give it a plot.
- Describe the figures. Who are the most active figures? How are they active? How is each officer concerned with a different member in the scene? (e.g., is there a positioning of high/low figures?).
- You will need to invent, but your story should contain the *logical* and *most probable* set of events that brought about the circumstances.
- Show care in the choice of words you use. Select words from the following list and use them in your narrative:

adequate	necessary	reasonable	requisite
satisfactory	suitable	disorderly	trivial
unusual	excessive		

  These words are often found in legal proceedings; to some extent, they are vague and even subjective, which allows for flexibility and judicial discretion. Try to use these words in a manner that best fits a standard of ethics and justice that the law requires or permits. For example, in using the word *excessive*, your sentence might be as follows:

  > In her statement to the police, the mother tried to dismiss charges, claiming that his abuse was not *excessive*, but merely the behavior of a temperamental man.

On the surface, it sounds simplistic to say that the main purpose in structuring a legal narrative is to persuade an audience of its truthfulness. Yet, success at persuasion requires a certain skill, such as recognizing the psychological (sometimes unconscious) reception of a narrative by the audience. This is because there is a stock of narrative that people internalize in their particular ordering of experiences. When hearing new narratives, people match them for reliability with those they have internalized. For example, if you were asked to recall the Da Silveira story (related early in this chapter), it would be doubtful that you would focus on the diplomatic immunity details of Article 29. Instead, you would likely connect it with a theme that matches the story (e.g., the abuse of a privilege) with similar ones in your memory. It is this identification with stock narratives and their themes that often sways jurors, judges, and the public at large. Although you cannot always predict how your narrative will play to the audience, its structure will certainly make an important difference.

EXAMPLE 4.5 A School Board Ruling

How, then, do we tell a legal story that would potentially result in some form of legal action? Here is an example of an actual controversy that took place in Muskogee, Oklahoma, in May 1996. The newspaper account (see Figure 4.2, p. 90) gives the facts as reported to the press. In short, the Oklahoma School Board had provided its high school seniors with a set of rules regarding dress codes for their forthcoming graduation ceremony. During the ceremony when diplomas were being distributed, three students walked on stage wearing "cultural symbols": One Native American had an eagle feather attached to her mortar board, and two African Americans wore kente scarves over their gowns.

The school officials denied the students their diplomas and transcripts unless they agreed to take a summer course as an instructional penalty. The students refused, with the following complaints: (1) their First Amendment rights of "symbolic expression" had been impeded upon and (2) their adornments proudly manifested their heritage. The school officials replied that the students had been informed of the code and that the board "wanted to bring back some level of dignity" to such a formal and public occasion.

Given students' natural impulses to identify with this episode, by virtue of their similarity in age and in their ideological leanings, I have used this story in class as an exercise in legal argument through narration. Since most of my students were inclined to oppose the school board, they were assigned the more challenging task of writing the narrative favoring the side of the school board. This forced them to structure their stories with several requisites: to be specific and cogent, to avoid inflammatory language, to justify their standards as a school

Diplomas Denied 3 Students Who Wore Cultural Symbols

By Lois Romano
Special to The Washington Post

TULSA, May 23—When Garrica Johnson chose to wear a multicolored African Kente cloth on her graduation gown last weekend, she expected to be prevented from walking across the stage at her high school ceremony. But she did not expect the call she received two days later.

Johnson and two other college-bound classmates, one African American and one Native American, were told by their vice principal on Monday that they would be denied their diplomas and transcripts from Muskogee High School for wearing cultural symbols on their cap and gowns.

To graduate and get their diplomas, Johnson; Sydney Watts, who also wore a Kente cloth; and Danaj Battese Trudell, who wore an eagle feather in her mortarboard, would have to attend a five-week summer school, the vice principal said.

Thus far, all three women have said they will not.

"I feel everyone has the right to express who they are and what they believe in," Johnson said. "The school system is trying to take that away from me."

The Muskogee school district, about 50 miles south of here, said the 18-year-old students violated a new graduation dress code—put into effect less than a week before the Saturday ceremony—that officials hoped would make the event more decorous.

Muskogee Schools spokeswoman Derryl Venters said today that all graduating students, including the three barred from diplomas, received letters informing them of the new graduation dress code a few days before the event. Venters said the students had attended a meeting where the policy was explained.

"The whole thing came up because the school district felt previous graduation services were a bit on the rowdy side," Venters said. "We wanted to bring back some level of dignity. Our way of thinking is that this policy is similar to other policies in this area relating to graduation."

But the American Civil Liberties Union believes the issue is one of students' rights and they said they would look into it.

"It concerns us that there were some students who wore visible Christian crosses and that was considered appropriate," said C. S. Thornton, an ACLU lawyer from Oklahoma City.

"Let me stress that we back the right of those students to wear crosses. But if that's okay, then why in the world would they punish these girls so severely? There's an impermissible discrimination going on here. People are being treated differently."

Johnson said in an interview today that she and her friends had expected to be barred only from the stage when diploma jackets were handed out Saturday (no one got the actual diploma that day).

When they were allowed to cross the stage, they assumed everything was okay, an assumption that was dashed with the call on Monday.

FIGURE 4.2 Newspaper Account of School Board Ruling

Source: Lois Romano, *The Washington Post*, May 24, 1996, p. A3. Reprinted with permission of the author.

board, and to answer the students' claims of protection as granted by the First Amendment.

The graduation ceremony episode was a complex instance of clashing values that basically leveled at right against wrong. Moreover, it involved the interpretation of arguments made by both sides. The Muskogee students' statements, given their age and status, were direct and simple. On the other hand, the school board's expressed wish "to bring back some level of dignity" contains more ambiguous wording. What is meant by *some level* or the term *dignity?*

The story, as presented by both sides, had opposite patterns of motives. According to those patterns, the narrative was structured into an argument. What follows is a student paper that champions the school board's position. It was delivered orally to my class and critiqued. It also contained a narrative of the research done to prepare the argument, which is included. As you read both parts, look for the ways this position has been structured and evaluate its success (or failure) in presentation.

Student Presentation

School Board's Position
on Graduation Ceremony

THE DISPUTE: To decide if the students were in the wrong and whether they should be granted their diplomas.

MY ROLE: I was appointed lead "defense attorney" for the Muskogee School Board. There were several ways my legal team (fellow classmates) felt that we should approach this case. Some felt that we should look into the legal precedents on separation of church and state cases. I felt that this was less a religious issue than a cultural one—although inquiries our team made to the Textile Division of the Smithsonian Institute in Washington, DC, indicated that the kente cloth may symbolize both religious and cultural identity. This was not a clear case of expressing First Amendment freedom of religion rights.

It seemed a better idea to contact the individuals involved in the event, since the names of key figures had appeared in the *Washington Post* account. Then we could get their own version of what happened. In addition, we could approach the ACLU (Oklahoma Headquarters) for *their* rendition of the case. In other words, "raw" or primary research would provide us with narratives of what different individuals believed had actually happened. [Certain names have been fictionalized to ensure confidentiality.]

THE RESEARCH: My first phone call was to Lois Romano, a journalist for the *Washington Post.* She was very helpful and gave me the number for the Muskogee School District switchboard. She even volunteered her opinions about the story, but I felt that since they were inadmissible evidence, they should not be included here.

My second phone call was to C. S. Thornton, an ACLU lawyer who was mentioned in the *Post.* His secretary said that he would get back to me. He never did. I will let you form your own opinion as to why he did not. I called the ACLU National Headquarters for information. The only information they were able to give me was that graduation dress codes are constitutional and legal. Also, that these codes are based according to region (local and state ordinances, which are in the *ACLU "Students' Rights" Handbook*, last published in its third edition in 1988). In this handbook, Oklahoma was listed as a state where the courts ruled that school officials are allowed to regulate, without justification, the dress and even hairstyles of its students.

I wanted to get to the core of this dispute and called the School District's switchboard. The operator, Mary Doe, seemed happy to give me details that had been omitted in the newspaper report. These details filled in the gaps which turned the whole issue around in favor of my team's side. Here are her details:

- The students had been told repeatedly about the dress code policy.
- Two assemblies were held, and students were spoken to individually, upon the students' own request.
- They were reminded of the consequences a final time just before crossing the stage at graduation.

Ms. Doe said that the Superintendent and the Principal and Vice Principal were standing there at the ceremony, to remind the graduating seniors. "They knew; that's why 241 out of 244 students got their diplomas," she said. She even gave me the following facts about what happened afterward. The three students decided to drop the case because they didn't think they could win. The suit never went to trial. She even gave me the "dirt" on two of the students. One of them was expecting a baby at the time of graduation and is now at home taking care of it. Another student enrolled in a college in Minnesota; this college offered him a full scholarship, even without the diploma. She did not know what had become of the third student.

Ms. Doe then directed me to Jane Smith, a secretary at the Board of Education, for further details. Ms. Smith said that "there was even a *student* committee on the dress code policy that went beyond the Board's policy, not only recommending it, but toughening it up considerably." This policy had yet another clause in it, one of those tiny clauses lawyers must love to find in such situations. The clause said that "after the students crossed the stage, were handed the diploma, after their hand was shook, and they did the traditional flip of the tassel signifying that they had graduated, they were allowed, *after walking down,* to display any cultural, religious, or ethnic garment, symbol, or item that they wanted."

This final piece of information was something I had planned to hold to the very end of the argument, when the opposition was growing tired and ready to rest their case. I knew that this little clause would win my case. I was now ready to put on my best suit and head for class to present my argument.

THE ARGUMENT:

Good afternoon, ladies and gentlemen of the jury. My name is Craig Goldstein and my job is to tell you the FACTS as I see them. By the end of the trial I believe that you will agree with our position. What we are going to decide upon was already decided in the Principal's office and the decision should have been left there. WHY? Because he has been given the authority to do so by the consent of the community and the direct power given to him by the Board of Education (who, let me remind you, you voted into office). And this type of decision is made in that office every day. For example, can students walk through the halls without a hall pass: NO. Can students use obscene language or fight on school grounds: NO. Can students wear eagle feathers or kente scarves on the ceremonial, traditionally approved graduation gown: NO.

This is a case about RULES BEING BROKEN. This is not about RIGHTS; this is about *following* rules, and in this situation *upholding* rules that were explained repeatedly. My opposition claims that the Muskogee school district officials should have been more compassionate to the students. But 3 out of 244 students, after fair warning, did as they pleased. This despite the fact that a *student* committee had toughened the policy even further. When rules aren't followed, there is chaos. Look at what happened in our community. We are getting national attention because of this debacle!

Dress codes have been around since the first schools in this country started having graduation ceremonies. Uniformity has made it possible to have a pleasant ceremony. Uniformity prevents others from feeling offended or being confronted. These gowns are supposed to be uniform. That's why the graduation march is the same across the land. That's why everyone wears the tassel on one side of the mortarboard, then flips that tassel to the other side.

No one person has the right to decide what is or is not acceptable. Would we want swastikas or KKK symbols displayed on the gown? We aren't denying anyone the right to express fashion or religious freedom. There is a time and place for that—but graduation isn't one of them. Remember, when seniors pick up their cap and gown, they do not find eagle feathers or kente cloths in the package. Therefore, members of the jury, the power is in your hands to decide this case by this important principle: in order to become responsible citizens, our youngsters must understand that rules are meant to be followed and upheld. Thank you.

Suggestions for Evaluating Student Presentation

- What is this student's thesis with regard to graduation codes? Is it supported by the narrative of accounts he gathered in his research?
- Cite one or two instances in which the account might be disputed by the opposition as unreliable evidence.
- Suggest any changes you would make to strengthen his argument that this is not a First Amendment rights issue.
- Discuss whether the use of narrative made this argument more interesting to read. More credible?

EXERCISES

4.1 *Narrative from Group Perspective*

Select a demonstration that you have read about or watched on television recently. Divide the class into the following groups: demonstrators, police officers, public onlookers, and newscasters. Then write a narrative about the demonstration from the particular perspective of your group. Compare the stories and decide which one rings most true. Discuss the means by which it succeeds in doing so.

4.2 *Narrative about an Experience*

Write a one-page narrative about an experience you have had or an event you have observed in which some aspect of the law was involved (e.g., being stopped for a traffic violation, watching an arrest take place, serving as a juror, visiting a corrections facility, etc.).

ENDNOTES

1. Bernard Jackson, *Law, Fact, and Narrative Coherence* (Liverpool: Deborah Charles Publishers, 1988).
2. *Jones v. Clinton*. Although the details of this case may be well known to the public, the Supreme Court's deliberations are grounded in a less-known government document: *Sexual Harassment in the Federal Workplace: Is It a Problem?* (Washington, DC: U.S. Merit Systems Protection, 1981).
3. "Immunity . . . Unsupported by Precedent," *The Washington Post,* May 28, 1997, p. A12.
4. Hugh C. Holman and William Harmon, *A Handbook to Literature,* 5th ed. (New York: Macmillan, 1986).
5. This is a fictionalized version of an account of the Cruickshank trial as discussed in Paula Diperna's *Juries on Trial* (New York: Dembner Books, 1984).

5

Writing the Argument

Guilty.	Innocent.
I did.	You didn't.
Your fault.	No, *your* fault.

How often do we hear such contrary positions unswervingly put forth? The legal profession exists in large part to settle disputes in which such contraries have not found resolution elsewhere. The best of such resolutions are achieved by skillful application of *argument,* a subject we will consider throughout this chapter.

As you read this chapter, be sure to consider any questions that might stimulate critical evaluation of the issues presented, and determine whether these issues have appeared in visual, oral, or printed form. For example, such issues may take the form of a witness statement (visual), a complaint (oral), or the terms of a contract (printed). Also keep in mind the basic purpose of your document. In other words, be clear in whether your purpose is to provide information, to persuade, or to record. For instance, your purpose may be to establish the validity of specific terms in a contract. Here, investigation of available facts will take priority; thus providing information will be the basic purpose of your document.

At the same time, an informative document may have an underlying intention to prompt or stimulate action without advocating that action outright. For example, suppose you are writing a report to a transportation administrative agency on the proposed installation of road bumps to slow traffic in a residential area. Although the purpose of these installations is commendable, drivers of emergency vehicles such as ambulances claim that the bumps actually cause injury to their passengers, who are already in serious condition. Your report, then, would serve a double purpose: to indirectly argue for some measures that will facilitate safety features and to find ways to address such contingencies as the use by emergency vehicles.

Facts, Opinions, and Expert Opinions

Your first job as a writer is to sort through those facts that will best support your position. You must ascertain which propositions in your material are indeed facts and which are merely opinions. In legal writing, facts will give more merit to your argument. However, there are instances when the use of opinion makes your point—especially for rhetorical effect. Therefore, it is appropriate to bring in opinions for emphatic purposes, but do so with discretion.

You may also encounter in your material statements that qualify as expert opinions. These help carry the weight of authority, especially if they are relevant to your point and refer to some legal rule or decision of importance. Although it is easy to recognize expert opinions, it is perhaps less easy to distinguish facts from opinions. Consider these differences:

- *Facts* are statements that can be objectively proved or disproved; they can be precisely defined.
- *Opinions* are statements that reflect the belief of the author and are intended as such in their context; they are statements that, by custom, are normally understood as opinions.
- *Expert opinions* are statements whose reliability is testified to by the recognized work and reputation of their author.

Using these criteria, identify each of the following statements as a fact, opinion, or expert opinion:

1. Zoning regulates the use of property, including the types of construction permitted within different zoning districts.
2. Senior citizens are entitled to financial protection by the government in their retirement years.
3. General Motors is the largest manufacturing organization in the world, with more than two million employees.
4. According to John Oberman, a forensic psychologist, "computerized control of the human brain is possible in the very near future."
5. Despite this nation's teenage drug-abuse problem, our young people are the hope of the world.
6. Lawyers who make high salaries are usually good lawyers.
7. A computer virus is a program specifically designed to cause harm; its user may be subject to criminal liability.
8. In his speech before the Senate, Senator John Lark said, "Industrial owners should be required to meet the new pretreatment criteria standards before they make sewage discharges."
9. One large bird can cause a crash on a 747 airliner if that bird becomes sucked into the jet engine.

Answers: Items 1, 3, 7, and 9 are facts; items 2, 5, and 6 are opinions; and items 4 and 8 are expert opinions.

Choosing Your Authority

When you organize your materials, it is wise to choose the best authority to support your argument. (See the Glossary for a definition of *authority.*) Use illustrations of authority (e.g., codes, statutes, ordinances, and rules); keep them focused so that your reader recognizes an applicable link between their provisions and your conclusions regarding the issue at hand. Your reader should not have to simply accept your assertions on faith.

Put yourself in the role of arguing a claim in which a client has suffered health problems brought about by a costly diet program. The client now seeks damages. You will try to establish authority by applying comparable facts from prior, similar cases to the present situation. Consider the following factors:

- *Similarity of facts:* No two cases will be identical. Therefore, you must distinguish the ways in which the main points of your authority resemble and differ from the main points in your case. Regarding the diet program, for example, what is the nature and sequence of events that led up to litigation in the former situation (your authority)? If there was litigation, what remedies did that client seek? Did the former situation involve the same diet program or one different from the case you are presently arguing? What was the actual outcome of the former case?

- *Level of court:* Assuming that there was litigation, at what level court was the case argued? It would be useful to learn whether the decision, if in favor of the client, was appealed to a higher court by the attorneys representing the diet program. Also, identify the specific language used in the claims that were made. This may include asking questions about direct cause, or *nexus.* That is, did the former case establish a direct, uncontestable blame of ill health to the diet program? If so, what was the legal terminology that defined or isolated such blame? How is it similar to your client's complaint?

- *Date of decision:* When did this prior litigation that you have chosen as your authority take place? Since diet programs in this country have acquired fad proportions, and since publicity for these programs seems to be mushrooming out of control, your argument should emphasize the legal consequences that result when customers' health is affected. Therefore, it is best to find the most recent case decisions on this subject. It is likely that more recent decisions will contain syntheses of earlier authorities and, as such, will indicate stronger punitive possibilities for your particular case. They may also lead you to additional, relevant, and seminal authority.

In short, choose your authority by these standards:

- Be sure the authority is pertinent.
- Select only that authority which is necessary.
- Cite from your authority those specific facts—and no more—that will support your argument.

Formulating the Thesis

A thesis for any argument goes directly to the main idea in order to establish direction and control over the material. It should make clear, without condescension to either side, what points are contested and what points are agreed upon. It should also address either side of your audience as intelligent and interested in your position.

The *formulation* of your thesis is determined according to the way in which it is worded and where it is placed in your text. Consider the following options on how to present your thesis:

- State your thesis outright as an aid to your reader.
- Avoid making a direct statement of your thesis, but marshal every detail so carefully that its underlying proposition is evident.
- Place your thesis statement in the beginning or the end of your text.
- Reiterate your thesis statement a number of times, each time with different examples, so that it becomes familiar to your reader.

One effective strategy for formulating a thesis is to present several standards or criteria to the reader regarding the feasibility of your position, as in the following:

- Can it be supported legally or constitutionally?
- Is it practical?
- Is it humane and morally justifiable?

Examples of Thesis Statements

The issue of legalizing marijuana for specific medical uses will serve as an example. The following thesis statements take these positions: Example 5.1 is in favor; Example 5.2 is in opposition.

EXAMPLE 5.1 In Favor

> Inasmuch as personal testimony by patients with AIDS, terminal cancer, and glaucoma has indicated that marijuana use provides relief from pain and has improved their quality of life, it is urged that action be taken to offer accessibility, through legal measures, to such individuals who would benefit from the legalization of marijuana for medical purposes.

The wording of this statement satisfies at least two of the preceding questions (e.g., Is it practical? and Is it humane and morally justifiable?). However, depending on your audience, you might add pertinent details to this thesis statement. For instance, you might tell a sympathetic audience that many physicians polled say that they would prescribe marijuana for such patients if it were to be legalized. If your audience is adamantly in favor of such legalization, you might note that some physicians admit they advise certain patients, in private, to use marijuana. Last, if your audience is opposed to the idea, ask them to imagine a scenario in which *they* or a loved one were to become afflicted by one of these diseases.

EXAMPLE 5.2 In Opposition

> If marijuana is such a helpful medicine, why haven't more physicians prescribed Marinol, the active ingredient in the cannabis leaf? It has been available for nearly two decades. If doctors administer Marinol (THC), patients are protected against carcinogenic agents in marijuana. Marinol has the endorsement of the Federal Drug Administration. If we allow the use of marijuana to be privately grown, we avoid the testing process so necessary to determining its safe consumption. We must protect millions of Americans by saying *no* to legalization.

This thesis statement answers the preceding questions by going directly to the medical alternative, which, though considered safe, is not widely employed. The statement also steers clear of questions regarding humanity and morality, sticking just to the scientific evidence. However, both of the thesis statements require amplification, since each position leaves certain factors unresolved. It is in the argument itself that those factors must be addressed.

Introducing the Argument

If your audience is fairly familiar with the issue and even recognizes it as a problem, the introduction or opening section of your argument will serve to remind them rather than convince them. Nonetheless, this is not a reason to omit stating what they already know. On the other hand, your position may constitute just one of several in a group of other recommendations known to your audience. Then you must take the time to refute rival recommendations and emphasize the preferred "do-ability" of your own recommendation. For example, one suggestion made by those who oppose smoking marijuana is to dispense Marinol, or THC, in prescription form. When a patient is given THC, proponents claim, we can be certain of its chemical components, whereas there may be dangerous, unknown substances in privately grown marijuana cigarettes.

The introduction is the right place to confront such arguments in the following ways:

- Offer data or statistics that discredit rival views.
- Provide anecdotal passages or personal statements from patients who testify to your position.
- Ask that your position at least be given attention.

Developing the Argument

As you develop your argument, consider what area of the law it will pertain to. Disputes arise in a number of different areas of the law, but common among the areas in which court cases will most likely result are crimes, torts, and contracts. Although it is not the purpose of this text to provide legal analysis of these terms, I will take one of the three, *crime*, and briefly state its classifications, since crime is the issue involved in our example of legalizing marijuana for medical purposes:

> [*Crime* is] a public wrong, committed with intent or by negligence, for which the law provides punishment or recompense to society. These are three common categories of crimes:
>
> 1. White-collar: nonviolent crimes, perpetrated by people in positions of trust, usually against business or governments.
>   Examples: embezzlement, mail fraud, bribery
> 2. Organized: crime by groups in the "business" of crime, such as the Mafia.
> 3. Victimless: crimes that are sometimes considered to have no specific victims (just society as a whole).
>   Examples: prostitution, gambling, tax evasion[1]

As you can see from these classifications, legalization of marijuana for medical purposes fits most readily into the third category. Hence, if your are advocating legalization, you must emphasize the need to remove the stigma of criminality imposed on those who would use marijuana for medical purposes. On the other hand, if you are opposed to legalization, you must emphasize the possibility that marijuana would fall into the hands of those close to the patients—especially teenagers—posing potentially dangerous consequences.

When you have completed your research, chosen or narrowed your issues, and settled on how to structure and order them in your argument, try to hone your materials down to those that are most indispensable. Avoid the superfluous and keep the following recommendations in mind:

- Select the best arguments for the issue(s) involved.
- Use just two or three of the arguments that you consider the strongest.

- Remember that an overload of issues may have two effects: Stronger issues tend to get lost in the crowd, and the presence of weaker issues tends to lead the audience to conclude that the entire argument is weak.
- Force your thinking into legal channels as much as you can; use the law as support whenever possible and applicable.
- Base your argument on one theme that runs through your document.
- Create a focus without seeming to do it directly or repeatedly, which can become annoying to the reader.
- *Shape* the best argument; the person who shapes the best argument generally wins the case.
- When the law is *not* in your favor, argue the facts.

By now, your background study and research should have accomplished the following:

- The existence of the issue or problem has been verified.
- The causes and effects of the issue have been analyzed.
- The evaluation, whether positive or negative, is specific.

Next, you must recommend a course of action that will either improve or impede the state of affairs that you have been examining. Ask yourself what specifically can be done to stimulate action for improvement, change, justification, or resolution of the problem. How to sequence your answers, remedies, and solutions in the most coherent manner is discussed next.

Initial Paragraphs of Your Text

You should not be afraid to appeal to the emotions and values of your audience (e.g., judge, senior partner, opposing counsel, etc.). However, this must be done with restraint; avoid arousing emotions to the point that it might deflect your audience from action. Your initial paragraphs are challenging to write. You are sending an immediate message to your reader as to whether you command respect, whether you sound credible, and whether you are qualified to write the position. Consider the following tips about writing your initial paragraphs:

- Write short, self-contained paragraphs that detail just one or two of your points in proper sequence.
- Avoid a headlong leap into the total scope of your argument.
- Delay full-scale ammunition until later in your paper, since a barrage of facts may be wasted if presented too early on.
- Emphasize *why* you are writing this position.

The initial paragraphs are also a good place to mention the criteria you will expand upon later in your argument (e.g., questions of safety; cost factors; risks and benefits to individuals, to the community, or to the nation; etc.). Remember that the early sections of your argument establish your voice; therefore, try to avoid rambling on or hammering readers with your message.

Transitional Devices

Your objective in developing an argument is to help your reader move easily from point to point. Thus, you need to make logical connections between these points. Think of your writing as a form of conversation, one that offers connectors or transitions for direct and clear comprehension. The following words and phrases help provide transitions as a way to express different meanings:

- *To establish purpose:* for this purpose, to this end, with this intention, to clarify
- *To emphasize:* of course, indeed, in fact, actually, in effect, most assuredly
- *To state results:* hence, accordingly, consequently, thus
- *To make comparisons:* likewise, similarly

- *To make qualification:* equally important, meanwhile, at the same time, on the other hand
- *To make addition:* first, second, further, in addition, moreover, lastly
- *To indicate time:* lengthily, immediately, in the meantime, at the time, now, at present
- *To indicate place:* nearby, beyond, parallel to, adjacent to, opposite to
- *To contrast:* however, nonetheless, nevertheless, notwithstanding, on the contrary, yet

Transitional devices have their place in every part of your argument. At the microlevel, they provide logical connections between sentences in a paragraph; at the macrolevel, when used at the beginnings and ends of paragraphs, they hold the argument together in a smooth, coherent fashion.

The following are two suggested paragraphs on legalizing marijuana for medical purposes: Example 5.3 is in favor; Example 5.4 is in opposition. They demonstrate the use of transition words for coherence. (*Note:* Transition words are underlined.)

EXAMPLE 5.3 In Favor

The U.S. Court of Appeals for the Fifth Circuit upheld the Bush administration's 1992 decision barring doctors from prescribing marijuana. At the time, that decision was supported by substantial evidence, the court claimed, noting that medical experts have testified that marijuana's medicinal value has never been proven in sound scientific studies. Now, the Clinton administration is reconsidering the ban. At present, only a handful of people have been granted permission to use marijuana, but new requests have not been approved. However, a Drug Enforcement Administration law judge believes there is substantial evidence of its usefulness in easing the effects of some illnesses. In sum, there are tens of thousands of people who want to use marijuana and thousands of doctors who want to prescribe it.

EXAMPLE 5.4 In Opposition

> Today's drug abuse is largely due to the breakdown of family units. <u>Indeed</u>, with broken families becoming the rule rather than the exception, and with communities being plagued by violent crime, teenagers have no parental or civic guidance about the dangers of drugs. <u>Hence</u>, teen pregnancy, domestic abuse, delinquency, and school dropout rates occur in settings where illicit drugs are located. <u>Consequently</u>, if legalization of "medical marijuana" were to be approved, thousands would be able to grow, use, and distribute it with a physician's recommendation. <u>To clarify</u>, there would be no measurable control over who would have access to the drug. <u>Thus</u>, we should not accept a substance that has shown to have minimal efficacy and maximal psychotropic effects.

Isolating Facts

Facts take on importance depending on their relation to other facts, cases, statistics, and the like. (See the Glossary for a definition of *facts.*) Therefore, the facts you choose for your argument will affect the perception of rightness or wrongness of your position. Here are some ways to isolate facts for effectiveness:

- *Enumerate facts:* Consider all the inferences that may arise from your facts. What is implied by these facts? (If they resulted in such and such, what would one conclude?) List the possibilities, the probabilities, and, if necessary, the unknowns.

- *Acknowledge the emotional significance of facts:* Bring in the real-life implications of your facts. (Could they result in injury, death, long-term psychological impairment, or disability?)

- *Place facts in context:* Refer to the issue's place in history, in a particular community, or in legal precedent. This can be done by identifying the *who, what,* and *why* that state the nature of your position.

- *Characterize facts objectively:* Select your wording in a manner that depicts persons or situations without prejudice (i.e., refer to a *one-*

time defendant rather than to a *known drug trafficker*). Use words like *just, fair,* and *legal;* they help to distance your personal judgments from more respected authoritative standards.

Avoiding Fallacies

One of the ways to strengthen your argument is to base all premises or statements on the validity of logic and reasoning. Errors in reasoning, known as *fallacies,* often derive from rhetorical or psychological appeals to the emotions. Fallacies have the potential to divert your audience from the matter at hand. They can also be used to make what is only seemingly true appear to be true. Although fallacies may be useful in some circumstances, such as in political statements, they have no place in legal writing. The following are some fallacies to avoid when writing your argument:

- *Hasty generalization:* This fallacy generalizes an idea or proposition that lacks the support of data, sufficient sampling, or adequate evidence.

  Example: People who use marijuana are committing a criminal act. Therefore, those who advocate legalizing marijuana for medical purposes have no respect for the law.

- *Non sequitur:* With this fallacy, there is no logical or valid connection between the statement and its conclusion. *Non sequitur* is a Latin term meaning "it does not follow"; therefore, the conclusion does not follow the statement or premise.

  Example: People who use marijuana for medical purposes will soon desire stronger psychotropic substances. Therefore, they will become heroin addicts.

- *Either/or fallacy:* Writers who use this fallacy suggest that there are only two alternatives or options in an issue or premise.

  Example: Either we say "to hell with it" and legalize medical marijuana for anything from migraines to toothaches, or we decide that it should not be legalized for any medical use.

- *Poisoning the well:* This fallacy generally takes the form of a question that requires an admission of fault even though this may not be the case. It is sometimes referred to as a *rhetorical question.*

  Example: Does the Drug Enforcement Administration have any idea how it distorts the scientific process when it engages in research regarding the benefits of legalizing marijuana for medical purposes?

- *Ad hominem fallacy:* This fallacy derives from a Latin term meaning "against the person"; it attacks a person's physical appearance, personality, or similar characteristic and ignores the person's actual views on the issue at hand.

  Example: I discredit the senator's views about legalizing marijuana for medical purposes. He is known to be a ladies' man, as well as a negligent parent.

Choosing Lines of Argument

The following lines of argument can be used to support your position:

- *Antithesis:* Find an example that is unrelated or opposite to your subject and use it to reinforce your claim.

  Example: We have no difficulty approving the use of mind- and mood-altering drugs (e.g., antidepressants) for mental problems or illness, yet these substances have the potential to cause dependency or addiction. How does this differ from approving the use of marijuana for medical purposes?

- *Cause and effect:* In this line of argument, you proceed from a known cause to a probable effect.

  Example: Politicians are wary of approving any kind of legislation that involves drug legalization, even for medical purposes. Anxious for reelection, they will avoid raising this issue with their constituents. The probable effect of this attitude is the postponement of intensive legislative investigation into the problem.

- *Exaggeration of effect:* If you want to argue that those who oppose your position are exaggerating its consequences as becoming dangerous to society, in general, provide an equally exaggerated idea that seems improbable because it is extreme.

  Example: If we allow that a situation could lead to disaster and should be prohibited, we must find an analogous situation and argue that it, too, should be prohibited. Therefore, since aspirin has been proven to cause stomach disorders, it should be declared an illegal drug, just as medical marijuana is now.

Summary of Argument and Conclusion

Both your summary of argument and your conclusion need little belaboring. By this stage of your writing, you should have provided all the supportive amplifications of your position. Therefore, you can briefly respond to opposing generalizations in an emphatic way. You can also use this section to state recommendations for handling the matter. This would include, when relevant, suggestions as to how your recommendation may lead to other, future developments that are ancillary to the issue. For example, if you are in favor of legalization of marijuana for medical purposes, you might emphasize that medical findings from a wider application for the use of marijuana will provide increased samplings. This could advance medical research in other areas of disease.

The introduction of your argument is the reader's first impression; the conclusion is the final impression. Remember the following points when writing the summary and conclusion of your text. They may not all be required but they serve as a checklist:

- Leave your reader well disposed toward you.
- Summarize the leading facts of your argument and emphasize the law that is in your favor.
- Arouse the appropriate state of emotion in your reader.
- Refresh your reader's memory.

Finally, although it is good rhetorical practice to make your summary and conclusion emphatic, the following pitfalls should be avoided:

- Do not use conditional words or sentences in the conditional mood (e.g., *should, would,* or *could*).
- Do not be tentative; use forceful wording.
- Do not resort to general legal or constitutional principles.
- Do not contest facts that you have already contested; rather, stress *why* your discussion of the facts is important.
- Do not use overkill; this can become a form of editorialization.

EXAMPLE 5.5 Argument Paper

Now that we have discussed the various criteria for writing an effective legal argument, we will examine a student position paper and observe how these criteria function. The paper is entitled "A Proposal for a Less Restrictive Virginia Abortion Law." The purpose of the paper is to urge Hope in Northern Virginia, Inc., to advocate for the adoption of a less restrictive parental notification for abortion law. Hope in Northern Virginia, Inc., is a social services agency that provides pregnancy aid to women. The student writer is off to a good start: She has identified her purpose with a clear and narrow focus and she has chosen an audience that will be sympathetic to her position, making them likely to consider her argument as cause for action.

A Proposal for a Less Restrictive Virginia Abortion Law

Introduction of Argument

Abortion is a controversial issue in the United States. Within the broad category of abortion, however, laws regarding minors are even more controversial. Many states are attempting to limit abortions by enacting restrictions for minors. Parental notification for abortion laws is an example of such attempts. In recent years, many states have proposed or enacted parental notification laws; Virginia is the most recent state to propose such enactment. Virginia is currently debating in its State House and Senate the conditions of parental notification laws and those already implemented in other states. The purpose of this paper is to urge *Hope in Northern Virginia, Inc.*, to advocate the adoption of a less restrictive parental notification law for minors.

Virginia as Subject of Argument

Purpose Statement

Provisions of Law

Here is a summary of what these laws mandate. Essentially, parental notification laws require that one of a minor's parents be notified of her intent to have an abortion, and then that parent must give consent for the procedure to be performed. Usually, the only alternative to parental notification and consent is judicial override. This occurs when a judge decides, for various reasons, to provide consent and will bypass the parental notification requirement.

Background on Laws

It may seem that this debate began rather recently. In truth, it began in the seventies. In *Planned Parenthood of Central Missouri v. Danforth* (1976), the Supreme Court held that a state may not require parental consent as an absolute prerequisite to a minor obtaining an abortion without providing an alternative to the parental consent requirement (Trenkner, 1983).

Legal Reference

It was also held in this case that a state cannot constitutionally allow parents, guardians, or a spouse of any woman, including a minor, to prevent an abortion for no apparent reason.

Yet, in *Ohio v. Akron Center for Reproductive Health*, it was decided that it is *not* unconstitutional for a state to require physicians to notify a minor's parents of her intent to have an abortion. Thus, each state is allowed to determine how restrictive its abortion laws will be.

Proposed Legislation in Virginia

Virginia's Abortion Laws

Returning to Virginia, here is a brief review of its legislative history on this issue. A parental notification bill was first introduced in Virginia two decades ago. However, it was tabled because of the standard political turmoil that arises during state elections and administrative turnovers. In 1977 the issue resurfaced and bills were passed by both the State Senate and House; however, each of the bills had different requirements. Now the Virginia General Assembly is in the process of reconciling the two before placing them on the ballot in the next election. Here are the essential points of difference between the Senate and House bills:

Current Status of Issue

Senate Proposal

Senate: Senate Bill #1096 was introduced on January 20, 1997. Section 18.2-75.1 considers a parent, a guardian, or a person standing "in loco parentis" authorized to receive notification of a minor who intends to have an abortion. However, unless the minor lives with a grandparent or adult sibling and it can be proven that the minor is controlled by that person, a grandparent or adult sibling is not considered an authorized person.

Qualifier in Bill

Senate Bill #1148 was also introduced on January 20, 1997. It more carefully defines an "authorized person." However, the definition emphasizes the juvenile court's role and authority regarding notification.

House Proposal

House: House Bill #2899 was introduced on January 20, 1997. While it also endorses the requirement of parental notification, it is less restrictive than the Senate Bill in several ways: (a) it states that the judge can determine if the minor is mature and capable of giving informed consent; (b) it states that an abortion can be performed without judicial approval or notification if a minor declares, or a physician suspects, that she is abused or neglected, and that abuse or neglect is reported to the proper channels. [Provisions a and b are actually amended versions of Bill #2899, added to section 18.2-75.3 on February 3, 1997.] These may seem to be slight changes, but they have a great potential impact on Virginia's minors.

Equally important, the House Bill did specify that a judge is allowed to determine the following: (a) if a minor is mature enough to give informed consent and (b) parental notification may be waived if it is in the minor's best interests.

Transition Paragraph

Arguments in Favor of Less Restrictive Laws

Psychologists and sociologists have conducted extensive studies regarding abortions for minors. Their findings support the conclusion that by age fourteen, most minors do have the cognitive ability to understand treatment options, compare the benefits and risks of having an abortion, and give legal consent. Additionally, they find that there is no scientific research supporting the contention that abortion has serious or lasting negative psychological consequences (Jones & O'Keefe, 1990).

Psychology Reference

Refutation

Moreover, there is an even stronger argument about the competence of minors to make decisions regarding abortion. In virtually every state, minors are allowed to use prescription contraceptives, are allowed treatment for sexually transmitted diseases, and are allowed pregnancy-related care. The only reproductive care a minor cannot always freely consent to is abortion. How is it that a minor is competent enough to consent to all of these reproductive health care services and not to abortion?

Rhetorical Question

Further Evidence

There is also a statistical argument which provides evidence that parental notification laws increase second trimester abortions for minors. Minors tend to have later abortions for several reasons: They take longer to recognize the signs or to admit to themselves the signs of pregnancy; and they have difficulty obtaining money for the procedure. For minors living in rural areas, there is the problem of travel cost and planning, as well. Thus, when a minor has been confronted with such delays, and is fearful of notifying her parents anyway, the parental notification laws may delay procedures further. In fact, 23 percent of pregnant minors under fifteen who have abortions will have second trimester abortions.

Statistics as Refutation

Transition to Connect Paragraphs

In sum, there are potential dangers for minors who wish to have an abortion and are subject to parental notification laws which are against their best interest. This is especially true when mandatory parental involvement leads to emotional and physical abuse of the minor, and statistics have shown that most pregnant minors come from dysfunctional families, where such abuse is often present (Boruch et al., 1991).

Conclusion and Recommendation

To conclude, it is not the purpose of this paper to champion abortion. Surely, sex education and more contraceptive services are more desirable alternatives to the problem of teenage pregnancy. But if we do concede that minors will continue to become pregnant and continue to have abortions, let us propose the most

Appeal to Audience

humane abortion laws regarding this population. *Hope in Northern Virginia, Inc.*, needs to advocate the adoption of a less restrictive parental notification law. That is, *Hope in Northern Virginia, Inc.*, as an organization which protects minor's rights, should draft an initiative for the Virginia General Assembly. At this point in time, the House Bill #2899 is the more fair and humane version of this law. Please inform the Assembly of your support for this version.

Plea for Action

WORKS CITED

Boruch, Robert F., et al. "Impact of the Minnesota Parental Notification Law on Abortion and Birth." *American Journal of Public Health, 81* (1991): 294–298.

Ginnow, Arnold., ed. *Corpus Juris Secundum,* Vol. 1. St. Paul: West Publishing Co., 1985.

Jones, James M., and Janet O'Keefe. "Easing Restrictions on Minors' Abortion Rights." *Issues in Science and Technology,* 7 (1990): 74–80.

Trenkner, Thomas R., ed. *American Law Reports: Annotations and Cases.* 4th ed., Vol. 23. New York: Lawyers Cooperative Publishing Co., 1983.

"Virginia General Assembly." *Commonwealth of Virginia NetServer,* 1997. House Bill 2899. Senate Bills 1096, 1148.

EXERCISE

Synthesizing Arguments

A final way to reinforce the points made in this chapter on argument is to explore the possibilities for synthesis. As you can see in the preceding student paper, there is a logical relation—or synthesis—between the ideas it presents. Since there is no one "right" way to synthesize material for an argument, this exercise will help you practice the mechanics of synthesis. Choose one of the following topics and write a 2- to 3-page essay in which you argue for *change.* In your essay, try to achieve an effective synthesis of your facts and arguments. Include in your essay the following components, all of which are discussed in this chapter:

1. At least one *fact*
2. At least one *expert opinion* (may also qualify as your *authority*)
3. A *thesis statement*
4. *Transitional devices*
5. A *line of argument* (e.g., *antithesis, cause and effect,* or *exaggeration of effect*)

Changes in the United States

A Change That Has Occurred	*A Change I Would Like to See*	*Reasons for the Change*
Suggested Topics		
Capital punishment	________	________
Affirmative action	________	________
Physician-assisted suicide	________	________
Sex offender community notification	________	________

Checklist for Writing an Argument

_____ Have you clearly stated the purpose of your argument?

_____ Have you included all the information that your audience needs and wants to know?

_____ Have you structured the document with appropriate signposts so that your information is clear?

_____ Have you attempted to resolve your argument through some form of alternative mediation or dispute resolution, rather than through litigation?

ENDNOTE

1. Robert Emerson and John Hardwicke, *Business Law*, 3rd ed. (Hauppauge, NY: Barron's Educational Series, Inc., 1997).

6

Research in Legal Writing

Part and parcel of doing legal writing is learning how to do legal research. This skill comes with practice and with knowing how to look for the right reference. This chapter provides a brief introduction to the sources and techniques of legal research with which you should become familiar. Later the chapter will walk you through a sample research exercise on a currently debated issue—mandatory uniforms in public schools. This exercise will demonstrate how you would search for the necessary materials on the subject of school uniforms, so that you would know the latest reliable facts—and law—for a paper on this subject. After you have absorbed the material in this chapter, your next step should be to go to a law library, immerse yourself in the stacks, and feel free to seek assistance from librarians.

Doing Legal Research

Researching a legal problem ranges from the broadest approach, called *background research,* to a more authoritative approach, *specific fact research,* which leads to *primary* and *secondary authority research.* Depending on the area of the law you are dealing with and the kind of information you require, you might use just one or both of these approaches, sometimes simultaneously. These approaches to research are *tools* recommended for use according to the level of research you will undertake.

Background Research

Often, when you have a legal subject to write about, you will not be familiar with its related terminology. Also, you may not know the main administrative agencies, courts, or levels of government that are procedurally involved in matters pertaining to your topic. Background research gives you a sort of general information, or overview, of the topic. It also provides the history of the subject, a selected coverage of its major issues, and probably some leads to both specific fact research and authority research, as well.

It is important to remember that sources used in background research are not considered authoritative and should not be cited in legal briefs. (Authoritative research will be explained in the next section.) An example of a background research source is the *ALR: American Law Reports* series, which contains articles that provide partial texts of selected court opinions. However, the chief purpose in providing these excerpts is to deliver extensive commentary and research on the issues addressed in these opinions. These articles also cite cases, which you can then examine if you need the complete text of an opinion. A better, more accurate tool, therefore, would be an official "reporter" that actually publishes the opinion. If, for example, you need the complete text of a Supreme Court opinion, it could be found in one of three volumes:

United States Reports, the only official reporter, published by U.S. Government Printing Office

Supreme Court Reporter, published by West

United States Supreme Court Reports, Lawyers' Edition, published by Lawyer's Co-operative Company

Specific Fact Research

Specific fact research is the method you will use when you need a primary or secondary authority (or source) that deals with the specific facts of your research topic.

Primary authority refers to any type of law that a court would choose to rely on in a decision-making process. Examples of primary authority include statutes, court opinions, constitutions, regulations, ordinances, executive orders, treaties, and administrative regulations. Their hierarchy is quite broad; that is, they will range from a Supreme Court opinion to an administrative agency regulation on worker's compensation (e.g., U.S. Department of Labor).

Secondary authority refers to any document that is *not* a law but may be used by a court to rely on in reaching a decision. Examples of secondary authority include legal periodical literature (such as law reviews), state bar association journals, manuals on legal practice, treatises, and legal encyclopedias. One of the chief benefits in using secondary materials is that they generally provide leads to primary authorities through extensive footnotes.

Doing Background Research

There is no more effective or persuasive authority than the citation of a primary authority in a courtroom; however, as a beginning writer in the legal field, you will more likely be assigned to do background research than to search directly in primary authority. Background research is a useful explorative process to learn, for it may direct you to higher-level sources. Some of the sources and techniques that will give you the background overview you will need are discussed next.

Legal Dictionaries

Be sure you have a good legal dictionary that contains all generic legal terms and phrases. In addition, if you are working in a specialized area of the law—such as the environment, education, or business—you can generally find a subject-limited dictionary for these sources, as well. Another possibility is to obtain a text on a specific area of the law that contains a comprehensive glossary of the terms in that area of the law (e.g., *Business Law,* 3rd edition, by R. W. Emerson and J. W. Hardwicke, Barron's Educational Series, 1997).

Your main purpose in consulting legal dictionaries is to find the officially agreed upon meanings of key terms in your research. It is also recommended that you get the most recent edition of a particular dictionary. Terms may change or vary slightly over time, especially if they acquire different emphases or new applicabilities through, for example, case or statutory law.

There are several more widely used generic legal dictionaries, such as the following:

Black's Law Dictionary

Ballentine's Law Dictionary

Law Dictionary, 4th edition, by Steven H. Gifis, Barron's Educational Series, 1996

Words and Phrases

(*Note:* The Gifis *Law Dictionary* listed here is an example of an updated volume with ample cross-references. It also includes in its Appendix such important texts as the Constitution of the United States and the American Bar Association Model Rules of Professional Conduct. *Words and Phrases* is a set of volumes whose definitions include excerpts from court opinions in which a particular word or phrase was pivotal, precedent making, or important to a legal transaction in some other way. Hence, it is a valuable resource for finding the original case in which usage of a certain word or phrase appeared in courts. It also indicates the purposes for which certain words and phrases have been used in certain legal matters. Therefore, *Words and Phrases* is not only an excellent guide to case precedent but it is also something of a "history" of the practice of the language of the law.)

Legal Encyclopedias

The two major national encyclopedias are *American Jurisprudence 2d.* and *Corpus Juris Secundum*. In addition, many individual states have encyclopedias that cover only their state laws, cases, statutes, and so on. For example, *West's Maryland Law Encyclopedia* provides a text summary of the rules and principles of Maryland law.

Both *American Jurisprudence 2d.* and *Corpus Juris Secundum* are supplemented by pocket parts as well as by revisions made to individual volumes; these serve the purpose of updating sources. In addition, these two encyclopedias provide ample cross-references to other cases, legal practice aids, and annotations or, in the case of the *ALR* series, commentaries.

Treatises

Treatises are books or multivolume sets of books written by private individuals on various topics of the law. They are similar to encyclopedias in that they sometimes give extensive coverage of the history of a legal topic (e.g., *Law in the Schools*, 1994). However, treatises differ from encyclopedias in that the former often give practical information on how to practice law in a given area. They function mainly as hands-on texts. The most common kinds of treatises are:

Formbooks

Practice manuals

Handbooks

These three types of treatises contain summaries of the law, offer sample forms for designated legal procedures, and provide checklists of essential component materials for different areas of the law. (An example of a manual directed toward those in the profession is *Practice Manual for the Maryland Lawyer*, which provides forms and how-to suggestions on practice details. It addresses common topics such as adoption procedures, name changes, and other subjects, as regulated in the st…
of Maryland.)

Another form of treatise is the *hornbook*, which also f… …on a
topic of law written by private individuals. Hornbooks … …y different from formbooks, manuals, or handbooks … are less
practice oriented and more devoted to covera… and commentary regarding particular topics of th… …e of a hornbook is *Law of Torts*, 4th edition, by … …lishing, 1971.)

Annotations

Annotation refers … Notes, and commentary
that may be ap… …ic law. Annotated reports
generally contai… plus notes or commentaries

on the opinion. When you are doing background research, you will often be asked to find out if there are any annotations on a particular legal point. The sources you will use are *ALR (American Law Reports, First Series), ALR2d. (American Law Reports, Second Series), ALR3d. (American Law Reports, Third Series), ALR4th (American Law Reports, Fourth Series), ALR5th (American Law Reports, Fifth Series),* and *ALR Fed (American Law Reports, Federal Series).* Since these sets of volumes contain appropriate excerpts of *selected* court opinions followed by extensive commentaries or research essays on the selected opinions, they are called *annotated reports.*

In a highly organized fashion, the *ALR* series provide all cases and all sides of the issue; the general principles derived from the cases; and the exceptions, qualifications, and applications of those cases. The *ALR* collections number among the most valuable research repositories in a law library; it is a good idea to familiarize yourself with them. Moreover, beginning with Volume 111 in 1993, the *ALR* series provide the following additional helpful items:

References to the frequently used West's *Key Number System*

References to the legal encyclopedia *Corpus Juris Secundum*

Search tools for databases compatible with Lexis and Westlaw, computer research tools

References to secondary sources such as law reviews

L[illegible] Periodical Literature

The[illegible]rally hundreds of law journals in the field. They are generally o[illegible]lity, since articles published in these journals are subject to peer[illegible] order to be accepted for publication. Inasmuch as these ess[illegible] written by law professors, attorneys, and administrative j[illegible] be relied on to contain official terminology, standard cit[illegible]ts, and other legal writing protocols. Many of these journ[illegible] *reviews,* are published by the major law schools in the [illegible] *Law Review*); some are published by state bar associa[illegible] *and State Bar Journal*); others are published by university interdisciplinary centers that utilize the law in their policy-making studies (e.g., *Law and Social Inquiry, Law and Society Review,* and *Law and Human Behavior*).

These different types of journals vary with regard to frequency of publication, some appearing monthly, some quarterly, and some biannually. Also, the level of authorship varies. For example, some law journals publish research essays only by the best students in their law school. On the other hand, state bar journals tend to publish essays by local practicing attorneys on current controversial issues in their own jurisdictions. For all these examples, it is understood that the opinions represented in the essays are those of the authors. Moreover, no legal periodical literature qualifies as primary authority. Nonetheless, this vast accumulation of legal scholarship offers valuable guides to research as well as cogent analyses of issues.

In order to locate legal periodical literature on your topic, go to one of these major indexes:

Index to Legal Periodicals

Current Law Index (print version)

LegalTrac (electronic version of *Current Law Index*)

Legal Resource Index

These indexes are extensively cross-referenced, allowing you to search for further materials under subjects that supplement your topic heading. For example, if you look up "Sentencing Guidelines" in the *Ind*
Legal Periodicals, you will be directed to these additional head act
rections, Plea Bargaining, Probation, Punishment, and ch of
Statements. Furthermore, *see also* references are pro
these headings.

Reports and Brochures

Background literature on th from a number
of less official resource chures. Sometimes
these publication positions on issues,
highlighting fact urpose of the agency

or group presenting them. Therefore, agency, committee, or association reports may not always score high with regard to validity, and should be read with discretion. The kinds of literature you can expect to find at this level of research include the following:

- *Agency reports:* Administrative agencies generally publish reports, newsletters, and pamphlets that are available to the public. They are useful for locating information on federal and state codes (e.g., public housing and tenancy regulations), as well as background literature.

- *Committee reports:* Before statutes are passed, they are discussed in special committees that prepare reports to present to the legislature. These reports are good sources of the legislative history of proposed statutes. If they are fairly recent, copies may be available by request. If they pertain to federal statutes, you can find them in the *U.S. Code Congressional and Administrative News.* "Legislative history reflects the background and events which lead to the enactment of a law. . . . [It is] useful to courts in determining the legislative intent of a statute" (*Black's Law Dictionary,* 5th edition, p. 810). This is why legislative committee reports are so valuable.

- *Reports of special-interest groups:* There are special-interest groups and associations for nearly every aspect of the law—health, welfare, environment, labor, tax, transportation, and so on. These groups constantly publish studies, position papers, and "white papers" that are available to the public. Such reports are obviously one sided, but they ... serve as useful source material for ascertaining the status of the ...ing sides on issues.

H... ...of Legal Types

Fine. Bu... utive ord... local or n... nonetheless? It's the LAW!

We intuit that this is not a treaty or an exec- ...lls us that this is probably some kind of ...—not terribly important, but a law,

As you approach legal research, you must have a sense of the different levels of the law, the kinds of laws that are operative, what their purposes are, and what their distinct peculiarities are. The following is a simplified list of legal categories, with brief explanations of their functions and intended goals. These types of categories can be found at both the state and federal levels. This list is far from comprehensive, but it does provide a hierarchical overview of the kinds of law you should know about in order to apply them to your research:

- *Opinion:* An *opinion* is the explanation or reason given for a judgment in a case. It is also known as a *finding* or a *conclusion* reached after applying a law (or laws) to the particular facts of a case. Opinions may be written by a single judge or by a three-member panel of judges, as in an appellate court.

Often, in Supreme Court decisions, Justices deliver *concurring* or *dissenting* opinions. Here, basically, is what is meant by these terms:

> *Concurring opinion:* Although there is a majority opinion written by a judge, several judges who agree with the opinion but disagree with the reasoning on which it was based may, for example, choose to refer to different case precedents as part of thei[illegible] reasons for concurring with the majority. Concurring [illegible]s generally appear as a supplement to the majority opi[illegible]. [illegible]ften, they become the subtle basis for reopening the ar[illegible]nt in a case with similar circumstances.
>
> *Dissenting op*[illegible] [illegible]ssenting opinions are in disagreement with the opi[illegible]d by the majority. They may disagree in part or in [illegible]isposition made of the case. Although these opinions [illegible] power in the decision, they appear in the text as a supple[illegible]. Moreover, as with concurring opinions, they, too, may serve in [illegible]e future to reopen arguments involving similar circumstances.

Dictum: It is important to include *dictum* as a separate subtopic under *opinion,* since it is a judge's view of what the law is or might be. The essential legal difference between dictum and the kinds of opinions just mentioned is that dictum is based on facts that are *not* before the present court. Therefore, dictum is not essential to the holding of the opinion.

• *Statute:* A *statute* is a law or act passed by either a federal or state legislature, such as the state of Maryland's law that prohibits the number of handguns a person may purchase. The purpose of a statute is to define and prescribe appropriate and inappropriate standards of behavior; to establish public and private provisions of these standards—from seat-belt laws to criminal codes—in accordance with constitutional authority; and to assure the protection of the individual. Although the terms *statute* and *act* are often used interchangeably, an *act* is the total set of categories detailed in the written document that contains the statute (e.g., the Civil Rights Act of 1964, as amended).

• *Constitution:* A *constitution* is the most important legal document that represents a system of government—whether it be a county, a state, a nation, a cluster of nations (as in the constitution of the United Nations). All the laws in any of these systems are subject to the authority of their constitution, which frames and identifies basic rights and obligations. In the United States, the Constitution is the supreme law of the land. In any state in the United States, the state constitution is the supreme law within that state. This basis for government continues in descending order to all jurisdictions (e.g., counties, cities, boroughs, districts, and wards). The relationship between the laws in each of these jurisdictions is subject to [illegible]ntinual adjustment. This fact is most observable in debates involving th[illegible]lation between federal laws and the laws of the states (i.e., state disputes [illegible]ssert autonomy from federal interference in their rulings).

• *Administrative regulations:* These [illegible] whose purpose is to define, explicate, and ma[illegible]s or other directives [illegible] These [illegible] statutes or executive orders by which an agency functions. [illegible] and act as gui[illegible]s are open to the public, subject to judicial review, [illegible] administrative agency hearings. For example, the U.S. Departme[illegible] ture has numerous regulations regarding the modes of proce[illegible] ufacturing, inspecting, and distributing all the produce consumed by the public. In addition, the department provides expl[illegible] sanctions that are mandated for violation of any of its regulations.

• *Charters and ordinances:* These kinds of laws refer to local units of governments. They are generally drawn up to give a certain municipality the authorization that makes a law applicable in that particular jurisdiction (e.g., bingo nights at the fire stations of a district, teenage curfews in an inner-city district, etc.). There is a slight difference between the two:

> *Charters:* A charter somewhat resembles a constitution in that it is the fundamental set of laws for a local unit of government. It designates specific accommodations, such as police, fire, hospital, and school services. It also describes specific governmental functions related to the orderly functioning of the community authorized in the charter.
>
> *Ordinances:* Ordinances are laws passed by governmental bodies below the state level. Therefore, there are county ordinances, district ordinances, ward ordinances, and so on. These laws generally deal with a local concern (e.g., water shortages, traffic intersection problems, pollution regulation, etc.).

Statutes and Case Law

Before we move on to the next section of this chapter, a brief note is needed regarding statutes and how they relate to case law. It is important to understand that while courts have the power to increase or lessen the scope of a statute, a statute may not be disregarded in case law unless it is determined (in rare instances) by a higher court to be unconstitutional.

Statutes originate at a legislative level and, when enacted, affect future case law. For example, if you are doing research analysis for a client, you will be required to compare categories described in a statute (or statutory provision) with the fact categories of your client's case. The greater their similarity, the more relevant the statute (or statutory provision) will be. Therefore, one of the most important skills to acquire in legal research is learning how to analyze statutory language and statutory definitions, and how various sections of a statute will determine applicability of certain groups or persons.

Kinds of Legal Authority

Earlier in this chapter, two forms of legal sources you will find in specific fact research were mentioned: primary and secondary authority. However, when identified in that part of the chapter, *primary* and *secondary authority* referred to examples of what to search for when undertaking specific fact research (e.g., an executive order or statute as primary authority; a legal encyclopedia as secondary authority). In this section, legal authority is taken one step beyond its research designation. Its function in the actual rendering of a decision by the court is explained.

Before discussing the function of legal authority, it is important that you understand the distinction between primary and secondary sources, because they serve different purposes. Some primary sources, for example, are key to making an argument in a formal court submission. On the other hand, some secondary sources are key in simply acquainting the legal researcher with a topic. Hence, the two types of sources in combination help define what is called *legal authority.*

Black's Law Dictionary defines *legal authority* as referring "to the precedental value to be accorded an opinion of a judicial or administrative body" (p. 121). This means that when you have litigation underway, your precedents will be determined by how closely they cover the facts of the present case. Such a distinction determines whether a primary or secondary authority is "on point" (*Black's*, 5th edition, p. 121).

Three types of legal authority will be discussed here: mandatory, persuasive, and nonauthority. We will also discuss how or when any of these types is on point (i.e., covers the facts of the problem you are researching). This will clarify why they are classified as primary or secondary authority, which helps you decide where to look when you do legal research. The three types are as follow:

- *Mandatory authority:* Mandatory authority is that kind of legal authority that a court or administrative body *must* rely on when it renders an opinion. It is a form of primary authority. As noted earlier, primary authority refers to any type of law that a court or administrative body *would choose* to rely on in a decision-making process.

  Example: A Second Circuit (appeals) decision is cited in a brief to the Second Circuit Court of Appeals.

- *Persuasive authority:* Persuasive authority is legal authority in nonmandatory primary authority or in any kind of second authority. Here is an example of nonmandatory primary authority:

  Example: Reference in a brief is made to a New York Federal District Court decision for a case before a Federal District Court in Maryland.

The following is an example of persuasive authority as secondary authority:

> *Example:* A law review article related to the facts and issue before the court or administrative body is cited in a legal submission to that court or administrative body. (*Note:* Although the use of this law review article may be used to influence the decision maker, the court or administrative body need not accept or consider this reference in reaching a decision.)

- *Nonauthority:* Nonauthority is legal authority with three different meanings:

> Digests and Shepards (research tools that allow you to help determine current validity of a law, whether it is a case decision, statute, constitution, administrative regulation, or ordinance), which are never relied on as authority themselves
>
> Primary or secondary authority that is not on point
>
> Primary authority that does not validly extend into the geographic boundary (i.e., geographic jurisdiction) of the court where you are in litigation (known as the *forum* court)

When you are conducting research on a legal matter, you must be familiar with these different types of authority in order to present the most cogent argument possible in a submission to the court or administrative body. A brief submitted to a court, for example, that has no mandatory authority, but only cites to persuasive authority or nonauthority, need not be considered at all by the forum decision maker. Further, a court or administrative body need only follow authority that is law, be it the federal (U.S.) Constitution, a state constitution, a state or federal statute, an executive order, a U.S. treaty, a precedental case decision, and so on.

Another factor that further complicates research of proper legal analysis is what may be considered mandatory in one jurisdiction or court may be only persuasive authority, or even nonauthority, in another forum. For example, an on-point opinion from New York's highest court interpreting that state's law would be considered mandatory authority for all of the lower state courts within New York state. However, if that same state law is applied by a Connecticut court, it would be considered persuasive authority. Also, if that same opinion cites a local ordinance from the neighboring state, then it would be nonauthority and of little or no legal significance. Thus, the legal authority you use to make an argument can literally make or break your case.

Sample Problems on Types of Authority

Here are some problems that deal with the types of legal authority we have just discussed:

PROBLEM 6.1

You have just filed a federal sex discrimination lawsuit in a California Federal District Court, which is a trial (lower) court. You have jurisdiction to file the lawsuit under the Civil Rights Act of 1964, as amended, a federal statute. List five examples of mandatory authority for this forum.

Answers to Problem 6.1

1. An on-point opinion of the U.S. Supreme Court interpreting the Civil Rights Act of 1964, as amended
2. A provision of the U.S. Constitution that is on point
3. A federal administrative regulation or decision that is on point
4. An on-point opinion from the same jurisdictional district
5. An on-point opinion from the U.S. Court of Appeals within the proper geographic area

PROBLEM 6.2

You have been asked by the senior partner of the law firm you work at to perform general background research on the issue of Fourth Amendment search and seizure. List three sources of nonauthority you can consult to begin this type of research.

Answers to Problem 6.2

1. *Corpus Juris Secundum* (*CJS*)
2. *American Jurisprudence 2d* (*Am Jur 2d*)
3. Any hornbook (treatise) on the subject

PROBLEM 6.3

You have just been retained to represent a young man in his personal injury suit before the trial court. He sustained injuries in a car accident while driving in the state of New Jersey. List three examples of *each* kind of legal authority you can use in researching liability issues in this case.

Answers to Problem 6.3

Mandatory authority: An on-point New Jersey state statute, an on-point opinion of the highest state court in New Jersey, and an on-point New Jersey administrative regulation

Persuasive authority: An opinion from another state court, an opinion from a higher than trial court but not the highest court in New Jersey, and an on-point reference in the *ALR* series

Nonauthority: A statute or regulation from a state other than New Jersey, a law that is not on point (e.g., the law may have facts that are distinguishable from the case at hand), and a parallel citation found in the Shepards

Sample Exercise on Research

Now that you are familiar with the major kinds of authority and legal research sources, this chapter will conclude with an exercise that demonstrates how to use a number of the sources that have been described. This is done by explaining how to search for materials in a particular legal research project.

Suppose that you have been assigned to write to a committee in the Maryland legislature at Annapolis. The purpose of your paper is to argue against mandatory school uniforms in Baltimore City. (*Note:* This topic was chosen for two reasons: (1) It is currently being debated in a number of state legislatures, and (2) a proposal to adopt a mandatory uniform policy was submitted to the Maryland General Assembly in February 1997 [see Figure 6.1]. That proposal was re-referred to the Committee on Education for further study and will likely be reintroduced before the Assembly in a future general session. The proposal [Figure 6.1] is an example of legislative writing, which makes this research assignment more realistic.)

SENATE BILL 818

7lr2871
CF HB 970

By: **Senator Dyson**
Introduced and read first time: February 10, 1997
Assigned to: Rules

A BILL ENTITLED

AN ACT concerning

Education — Public Schools — School Uniforms

FOR the purpose of requiring the county boards of education and the Board of School Commissioners of Baltimore City to implement the use of school uniforms by all students in the public schools by a certain date.

BY repealing and reenacting, with amendments,
Article — Education
Section 4–108 and 4–304
Annotated Code of Maryland
(1997 Replacement Volume)

SECTION 1. BE IT ENACTED BY THE GENERAL ASSEMBLY OF MARYLAND, That the Laws of Maryland read as follows:

Article — Education

4–108.

Each county board shall:

(1) To the best of its ability carry out the applicable provisions of this article and the bylaws, rules, regulations, and policies of the State Board;

(2) Maintain throughout its county a reasonably uniform system of public schools that is designed to provide quality education and equal educational opportunity for all children;

(3) Subject to this article and to the applicable bylaws, rules, and regulations of the State Board, determine, with the advice of the county superintendent, the educational policies of the county school system; [and]

FIGURE 6.1 Example of Legislative Writing

(4) Adopt, codify, and make available to the public bylaws, rules, and regulations not inconsistent with State law, for the conduct and management of the county public schools; AND

(5) NOTWITHSTANDING ANY OTHER PROVISION OF LAW, IMPLEMENT THE USE OF SCHOOL UNIFORMS BY ALL STUDENTS IN THE PUBLIC SCHOOLS IN THE COUNTY BY THE BEGINNING OF THE 1998–1999 SCHOOL YEAR.

4–304.

(a) Subject to the applicable provisions of this article, the Board of School Commissioners of Baltimore City may:

(1) Examine, appoint, and remove teachers;

(2) Set teacher qualifications;

(3) Subject to the approval of the Mayor and City Council, set teacher salaries; and

(4) Select textbooks for the public schools in Baltimore City, except that the textbooks may not contain anything of a sectarian or partisan character.

(b) (1) The Board of School Commissioners shall report annually to the State Board on the condition of the schools under its jurisdiction.

(2) The report shall include a statement of:

(i) Expenditures;

(ii) The number of children taught; and

(iii) Any other statistical information the State Board requires.

(c) NOTWITHSTANDING ANY OTHER PROVISION OF LAW, THE BOARD OF SCHOOL COMMISSIONERS OF BALTIMORE CITY SHALL IMPLEMENT THE USE OF SCHOOL UNIFORMS BY ALL STUDENTS IN THE PUBLIC SCHOOLS IN THE CITY BY THE BEGINNING OF THE 1998–1999 SCHOOL YEAR.

SECTION 2. AND BE IT FURTHER ENACTED, That this Act shall take effect July 1, 1997.

EXPLANATION: CAPITALS INDICATE MATTER ADDED TO EXISTING LAW.
[Brackets] indicate matter deleted from existing law.

FIGURE 6.1 Continued

Here are some basic steps for accessing information on the general legal status of the school uniforms issue. In order to write persuasively about proposed legislation for Baltimore City, you should first have information regarding the current national status of the issue.

How to Start

Begin by asking some general but directly related questions regarding mandatory school uniforms, such as the following:

- What are the possible legal issues that might arise when the state requires its county boards of education to implement the use of school uniforms by all students in their public schools?
- What are the general principles governing the prescribing of particular attire in public schools?
- What are the most important cases governing the prescribing of particular attire in public schools?

These are important questions because the general understanding is that uniforms may become required in a particular jurisdiction—in this instance, Baltimore City. However, the application of any rules that authorize mandatory uniforms could result in litigation supported by an activist association—such as the American Civil Liberties Union, which will plead First Amendment violation—and appeals by community groups that exceptions be made for children in poor families, resulting in local or county fiscal disputes regarding fund allotment. Both of these possibilities can be discussed through the use of terminology and case precedent in related cases pertaining to what is allowable regarding dress codes in education.

EXAMPLE 6.1 Case Precedent

In *Tinker v. Des Moines Independent School District 393* (US 503, 21 L Ed. 2d 731, 89 S.Ct. 733), students claiming freedom of expression wore black arm bands to school in protest of the Vietnam War. The school said such action was prohibited. The Supreme Court decided against the school board, claiming that this was a form of symbolic expression protected by the First Amendment.

In this example of *Tinker v. Des Moines*, is the precedent a *primary* or *secondary* authority for your present investigation into mandatory uniforms? Explain your answer.

Where to Look for Relevant Information

Rather than immediately searching for cases and precedents, as well as for political precedents in other parts of the country, you would do well to use general reference works—such as legal encyclopedias, annotations, and digests—to learn the terminology and identify the primary case authorities. Here is a suggested search process for finding information on mandatory school uniforms in these general reference works. It is also an item-by-item listing of what you will find.[1]

The best way to familiarize yourself with what follows is to look for each of these references in a law library and follow the search steps, as directed, in their sequential order. You should get the same results as those following the listings (e.g., you should not find an entry under "Uniforms" in *American Jurisprudence 2d.*). Also, as you may discover, you frequently need to try a number of different categories before locating the desired information.

Encyclopedias

American Jurisprudence 2d. To search for information relevant to school uniforms, look in the General Index under the following subjects:

"Uniforms" (no entry)

"Dress": See "Clothing"

Scan under "Clothing" (no entry)

Scan under "Schools" (no entry)

Scan under "Dress and Grooming Regulations": You see a reference to "Schools, §265."

Go to Volume 68, "Schools, §265," "Dress and Grooming Regulations"

Now that you have found the entry that satisfies your search, note its footnote references to cases and practice aids. Then check the pocket part of Volume 68. Notice that this may add later citations and other sources in these categories:

Case authorities (e.g., *Tinker v. Des Moines*)

Practice aids (e.g., sample litigation forms)

Practice references

Corpus Juris Secundum. Go to the entry for "Schools and School Districts." Scan for the following possible entries:

"Dress" (no entry)

"Clothing" (no entry)

"Pupils": There is an entry on "Free Speech and Expression." Reference is to "Schools and School Districts," §790. See pocket part. Note for future reference "Schools Key 169" (this refers to the West key number listed below under *West's General Digest*).

Annotations

Another valuable, even indispensable, resource for the legal writer and researcher is the collection of annotations in *American Law Reports* (*ALR*). The signed essays in these annotations analyze cases in relation to specific topics. You can find citations to reports you are looking for in the encyclopedias and in online services. However, an easier way to search for relevant annotations is to use the *ALR*'s own index volumes. Here is how to search the *ALR* index for information on school uniforms:

ALR Index

Look under "Schools and Education."

Find cross-reference to "Dress or Grooming Requirements."

Scan under "Dress or Grooming Requirements": You will see a reference to "Schools."

Scan under "Validity": You will find information in 14 *ALR3d*, 1201. (Note that the annotation covers pages 1201–1204.)

Under the heading "Total Client Service Library References," the editors of *ALR* add other resources regarding this topic, including a form for filing a complaint:

> 18 *Am Jur Pl & Pr Forms,* Schools, Form 18:141. (Note that this common abbreviation stands for *American Jurisprudence Pleading and Practice Forms Annotated.*)

Finally, examine the Update supplement pocket part in the back of the volume, listed under 14 *ALR3d.* 1201–1204. (Note that the original annotation was published in 1967. By 1997, the list of Research References in the Update had reached 12 pages. This suggests that the topic has taken on increased significance and coverage in legal research.)

West's Digests

Another useful search source are digests, which are volumes containing small paragraph summaries of court opinions. They are organized by subject matter, and their primary purpose is to serve as case finders. The major publisher of digests is West, which has a key number system that classifies the small paragraph summaries of the opinions in the digests. Every topic and subtopic in the law is assigned a key topic and number by West.

Regarding your search topic, *school uniforms,* you may use the regularly updated digests for a survey of current cases that may have relevance to our research. In order to see how this is done, examine the recent volumes of *West's General Digest.* Note that there are sequential series, such as:

> Eighth series, 1991–1996
>
> Ninth series, 1996–

Here is the way to search for your topic in *West's General Digest:*

Search each volume by using the West key numbers for the classification under "Schools." These are suggested numbers:

> #169 "Control of Pupils and Discipline in General"
>
> #170 "Rules and Regulations"
>
> #172 "Reasonableness and Validity"

You will not find references relevant to "Dress" or "Grooming" in each volume. However, they do appear in the key number entries (e.g., #169, #170, #172) in the following volumes:

Eighth series, volume 55 (1995)

Eighth series, volume 59 (1996)

Ninth series, volume 9 (1997)

These entries will provide your most direct lead to the information you will need.

As you have seen from this walk-through process, by examining legal encyclopedias, the *American Law Reports,* and the *West's General Digest,* you can learn what these secondary sources will provide as background materials, legal terminology, and the identification of the primary case authorities. Other secondary sources include articles in law reviews. However, searching for these and getting access to them is not such a direct process.

To conclude this overview, there are several other aids to accessing secondary sources that publish information dealing only with education law. The following provide further information on school uniforms:

Education Law This loose-leaf publication provides summaries of the law for school administrators. Here is a hint for searching in *Education Law*: Use the Index in Volume 4; look for "Dress Code."

Law in the Schools, W. Valente (Columbus, OH: Merrill, 1994). Here is a hint to help you in your search: Look for "Appearance and Dress" (p. 280) and look in Notes on p. 322 for other cases.

Electronic Search

A number of means of electronic research are also available (e.g., Lexis, Westlaw, Internet). For this school uniform exercise, we will use Lexis as our example. If you have access to Lexis and are familiar with road-mapping your way through its files, Lexis will supplement information you have found in other sources. Here, briefly, are some steps you can take to facilitate your search:

Begin with a known case name: *Tinker v. Des Moines*

Search GENFED, US

Name (tinker and des moines)

Note use of guide: .gu

From case citation: 393 US 503

To update the case, Shepardize in LEXIS: shep

EXERCISES

6.1 *Mandatory Authority*

You are a federal Social Security administrative law judge, empowered to enforce the regulations of the Social Security Administration and render decisions on administrative appeals to the Social Security Administration. In what court are your on-point decisions mandatory authority?

6.2 *Mandatory versus Persuasive Authority*

You are an administrative law judge for the state of New Jersey. In which states are your decisions mandatory authority? Are your decisions persuasive authority in other states?

6.3 *Index Terms*

Using law resources discussed in this chapter, search for the following topics by consulting the suggested *index terms* as possible locators. (*Note:* If you are looking for regulations that are pertinent to a specific state, it is a good idea to check the *Annotated Code of* _________ (name state) as well as the legal encyclopedias, annotations, and digests.)

- Juveniles charged as adults in the courts
  Index Terms: Juvenile Causes, Jurisdiction, Waiver of Jurisdiction, Juvenile, Jurisdiction
- Sex offender notification laws
  Index Terms: Sexual Offenders, Registration

- Physician-assisted suicide
  Index Terms: Right to Die, Euthanasia, Health Care Decisions
- Affirmative action
  Index Terms: Discrimination, Racial Minorities, Labor and Employment
- Same-sex marriages and adoptions
  Index Terms: Marriage, Validity, Adoption

6.4 *Using* Words and Phrases

American Jurisprudence Pleading and Practice Forms Annotated contains a Form 176 that is used in school procedures that enjoin the expulsion of a student for failure to conform to the grooming code. The representative who acts for the benefit of the juvenile (legally designated as "infant") is referred to as *next friend.* Actually, this representative is not a "friend" as the word is commonly understood but an officer of the court. Look up "Next Friend" in *Words and Phrases* for a background of the usage of this term in the law. Also, look up the following cross-references under "Next Friend" to see what additional information they may provide:

Committee

Guardian

Guardian Ad Litem

6.5 *Law Journal Articles*

This exercise requires you to read and digest a number of points of view from law journal articles regarding gun control. A list of such articles is provided at the end of this exercise.

Divide your class into teams (preferably five to a team) in which each student searches for and reads one of the articles listed. Each team member will write a 200- to 300-word summary of the article. When this phase of the work is completed, the team then compiles the summaries and has the team leader present a two- to three-page report on the articles read. The report should include:

- The point of view of the author of each journal article
- A review of the legal interpretations presented in the article
- The strengths and weaknesses of each position

Suggested Articles on Gun Control

Aborn, Richard M. "The Battle Over the Brady Bill and the Future of Gun Control Legislation." *Fordham Urban Law Journal, 22* (1995).

Brown, Wendy. "Guns, Cowboys, Philadelphia Mayors, and Civic Republicanism: On Sanford Levinson's *The Embarrassing Second Amendment.*" *Yale Law Journal, 99* (1989).

Johnson, Nicholas J. "Shots across No Man's Land: A Response to Handgun Control Inc.'s Richard Aborn." *Fordham Urban Law Journal, 22* (1995).

Larish, Inge Anna. "Why Annie Can't Have a Gun: A Feminist Perspective on the Second Amendment." *University of Illinois Law Review, 2* (1996).

Van Alstyne, William. "The Second Amendment and the Personal Right to Bear Arms." *Duke Law Journal, 43* (1994).

6.6 *Law on the Internet*

The following list could be called a "webliography." Check out these sites and make a brief annotated review of the legal areas they cover:[2]

- American Bar Association
  www/abanet.org
- Constitution, U.S.
  www.access.gpo.gov/congress/senate/constitution.toc.html
- Documents: Avalon Project
  www.yale.edu/lawweb/avalon/avalon.htm

- Federal law: Fedlaw
  www.legal gsa.gov/
- History and philosophy, legal
  www.commonlaw.com
- Law reviews and journals
  - Findlaw (full text search)
    www.findlaw.com
  - Law reviews on the Web
    www.lawreview.org/
- Legal news
  legalNews.FindLaw.com/
- Law professors' home pages
  jurist.law.pitt.edu/
- State codes
  see FindLaw State Resources indexes
- State and local government pages
  Piper Resources
  www.piperinfo.com/state/states.html
- Supreme Court (1937–1975)
  FindLaw
  www/findlaw.com/casecode/supreme.html
  www.access.gpo.gov/sudocs/supcrt/
  www.fedworld.gov/supcourt/index.htm

ENDNOTES

1. This section on using reference works was contributed by Robert Merikangas.
2. This list of websites was contributed by Robert Merikangas.

APPENDIX A

Advancing in the Field: The Application Process

This appendix covers the procedures and types of documents generally required for applying to law school, but it is equally applicable to those of you who plan other short- or long-term occupations related to the legal field (e.g., an internship in an administrative office or law firm, a paralegal position, or a legislative aide position). The objectives for all these positions are similar, despite the fact that variations regarding eligibility will depend on what area of the profession you select. Whatever placement you are seeking, all or some of the following documents and procedures are most often required:

- The application essay
- The letter of application
- The resumé
- The interview

For each of these documents, you must bring strong communication skills to the process. You will be judged by your written, oral, and personal presentation. Remember that what you write, what you say, and how you say it should establish your credibility as a person of intelligence, good character, and common sense.

Admission standards in both academia and the workplace are high. The guidelines given here provide sample worksheets and formats to help you meet those standards and to develop an effective presentation. For the most part, student samples are used. Some are poor; they serve as instructional tips on what *not* to do. Some are of good quality; they serve as suggestive models for a "best advantage" submission. However, before addressing these guidelines, three topics are provided for your consideration regarding your preparation for entering the legal field. These three items will help you plan your academic studies and make future commitments:

1. *Choice of major field of concentration:* If you plan to enter law school or a law-related field, there are many options regarding your major. The traditional choices made by students interested in law are courses in the humanities (e.g., English language and literature, political science, history, criminology, sociology, and psychology), but there are equally valid and useful nontraditional choices (e.g., speech, economics, business, African American studies, women's studies, and computer science). It is prudent to select a major that strongly complements your interests and skills, allowing you to do your best work. At the same time, if you have already decided on a certain area of the law, specialize in a related discipline (e.g., if you are interested in patent law, consider a major that entails strong technical training, such as engineering).

2. *Development of skills:* These are the essential skills to develop in your preparation:

   a. Written and oral communication
   b. Analytical and logical reasoning
   c. Reading comprehension

Take courses that require substantial reading, writing, and analysis of texts. Also take speech and argumentation courses (e.g., mock-trial courses) to help you perform well in oral preparations and debates. Another recommendation is to take a logic course for practice in critical thinking and decision making. Finally, try to build a foundation of knowledge through courses that deal with American political/cultural history, institutions, and values. (I require my students to familiarize themselves with the Constitution and to memorize the first Ten Amendments.)

3. *Extracurricular activities:* Active participation in student and community organizations will help you develop skills in leadership and advocacy. If possible, become involved in prelaw societies, moot-court teams, volunteer work with legal aid offices, various rights groups (e.g., Amnesty International or ACLU's student branches). These will add impressive items to your resumé. They also serve as excellent ways for you to discover the area and extent of your own interests in the law.

The Application Essay

There is no uniform policy that requires you to submit an essay with your application; some law schools or career-related institutions require an essay, others do not. For those that do, you may be given a specific topic to write on, such as the following (recent examples assigned by law schools):

- Discuss your view on the "English only" initiative.
- Who do you consider to be the greatest current political leader in the United States? Why?
- Discuss certain legal problems in your community that deserve immediate attention.

Perhaps you will be asked to submit an essay on any subject you choose or on that elusive phenomenon known as the "career goals" essay. Whichever of these is requested, here are several pointers:

- *"No man is an island":* Present yourself as an individual who participates in and cares about your community and society. Avoid overemphasizing your achievements or giving excessive self-praise; modesty draws its own praise.
- *Vary your self-presentation:* If your application is supplemented by transcripts or a resumé, do not reiterate the information provided in these documents. Let your essay reveal other information that may not be found elsewhere.
- *State your desire to contribute:* Tell the reviewers or the admissions committee the *specific* ways in which you believe you can serve the profession.

- *Avoid politicizing:* Steer away from writing about topics that are currently sensational or otherwise difficult to address with objectivity. Express opinions consistent with general ethical goals and fairness.
- *Avoid cuteness:* Although wit and humor are said to carry the day, what you think is funny may not be so to your reader. If you do incorporate a humorous anecdote or observation, do so with awareness of and sensitivity to diversity.
- *Be creative:* Your application will likely be in competition with numerous others. If you can provide a unique or original slant on your material, it may stand out in the pack, but you should be *cautiously* creative. (Admissions committees have been known to receive applications in which a shoe was enclosed, with the accompanying essay theme: "How to Get Your Foot in the Door." As you can imagine, this was not appreciated.)

For some students, writing an essay is the easiest task to perform in the admissions process. For others, it is the most horrific of chores. Following are several student essays that I have received in Legal Writing classes. They have been selected on the basis of the principles just discussed. As you read them, pretend you are on the committee that reviews such documents and make your own assessment.

EXAMPLE A.1 Student Application Essay

Application to the West Virginia College of Law

There are a number of reasons why my application to the West Virginia College of Law should be reviewed favorably by this committee. These reasons include my grade-point average throughout college, my prior experience in the field of law, and such intangibles as my desire and will to learn. Most important, the committee should take into account my intentions concerning my future career plans. These plans consist of making effective legal services available to all citizens regardless of their station in life.

I am currently a Government and Politics major in my junior year at the University of Maryland. My cumulative grade-point average of

3.72 demonstrates my dedication to academic achievement and excellence. Furthermore, my grade-point average has steadily increased from 3.0 to 3.8 over the past four years. I am currently a member of the Phi Kappa Sigma Honor Society and I have earned academic honors each of my four semesters at Maryland.

Concerning my previous experience in the field of law, I interned for Judge Calhoun, Head Judge in a local county Circuit Court, while in my senior year of high school. I was responsible for organizing and updating the court records and the court calendar. The internship allowed me to gain invaluable experience in courtroom affairs and legal decision making. In addition to the internship, I worked as a consumer loan adjuster and collector at a local bank this past summer. Since my duties included repossessing automobiles and boats, I had many opportunities to interact and negotiate with attorneys. As a result, I feel confident in dealing with attorneys and speaking their "language."

My desire to become an attorney began when I was a teenager, the same time my mother entered law school. I became fascinated with the different cases and conflicts we would discuss. As she helped me to better understand the law, she also taught me to appreciate and respect it. Watching her succeed in law school has only intensified my desire to follow in her footsteps.

Finally, I feel it is very important to make the committee aware of my future plans. Unlike many of today's law students, I am concerned more with justice than with money. Once I have graduated from law school, I plan to select the opportunity that will allow me to provide effective legal services to all citizens regardless of their income.

I would be an excellent candidate for West Virginia Law School because I have demonstrated dedication to academic achievement and excellence, and determination in pursuit of my goals. I am certain I will fulfill the expectations of and make a significant contribution to the law school class of which I am a member.

Evaluation of Student Application Essay

This student essay contains a number of problems, for which the following revisions are recommended:

- *Tone:* The general tone of the essay needs to be changed to avoid being offensive to the reviewer. What emerges from the writing is an image of an individual who holds himself above other law school students (e.g., "Unlike many of today's law students, I am concerned more with justice than with money"). Indeed, the admissions committee reviewer is very likely a lawyer; if so, this reviewer is indirectly being derogated as one of those who values money over justice. The student needs to eliminate this self-righteous tone.
- *Self-emphasis:* There are over 40 first-person pronouns (*I, me, my*) in the essay. This gives the impression that the student has a greater interest in himself than in the law school or what he may be able to contribute to that particular institution. A better tactic would be to name the special-interest areas the school curriculum offers (e.g., mental health legislation or minority rights legislation) and to express a desire to focus on that area whose goals the student wishes to promote.
- *Redundancy:* The first and last paragraphs of this essay, as well as certain phrases throughout the essay, are repetitive (e.g., "dedication to academic achievement and excellence"). A good essay is comprehensive yet concise.

EXAMPLE A.2 Student Application Essay

Application to Law School

In my years as a student at the university, I have found several concepts and areas of study to be somewhat difficult. For example, when I was a freshman I had a great deal of trouble understanding the botanical study of miosis. As a sophomore, statistics gave me horrible headaches. In my junior year, symbolic logic gave me indigestion. Yet, regardless of my difficulties in these classes, I eventually came to understand them. There were always answers to my questions and solutions to the problems.

There is one concept, though, that has continued to baffle me. That concept is "it." "It" has been mentioned in all of my classes, most of my reading, and even in slogans and commercial advertisements that I have seen or heard. My teachers have abstractly theorized about "it" in their lectures, leaving it up to me to discover its true meaning.

As a child, I was absolutely convinced that Coke was "it," until Pepsi told us that "it" was the choice of the next generation. Even as a young child I was confused over the meaning of this word. So, when I got to college I decided that this would be the perfect setting in which to discover what "it" is. I went to my philosophy professor for advice. He explained that since anything could be referred to as "it," "it" could be anything I wanted it to be. I thought of the commercial promoting the *Washington Post*, which reads, "If you don't get it, you don't get it." Nice play on words, and a great way to sell a newspaper.

So I decided to follow the adage "If it ain't broke, don't fix it," and only make adjustments to my views and actions when "it" doesn't seem right. I plan on sticking with "it" because when "it" seems just and right to me, I will follow the advice of Nike and "Just do it." Now that the concept is a little clearer to me, I regard it as a kind of truth table to carry me through law school. Then, hopefully, I will make the most judicious decisions for myself and for the welfare of society.

Evaluation of Student Application Essay

- *Tone:* This essay has an original theme, playing on a single word in a variety of humorous and commonly recognized contexts. More important, however, it underscores this student's ongoing thirst for knowledge and understanding. Its tone suggests that the student will take life's events and actions seriously—with a sense of personal responsibility. Yet the essay remains light and witty. It avoids a ponderous mood of pessimism regarding society; it also avoids a sense of messianic mission.

- *Self-emphasis:* Given the uniqueness of the essay, the student manages to draw attention to himself, but in a positive way. There is no grandstanding or boasting about accomplishments. Rather, he gives the impression that any challenge he faces will be handled with maturity and careful reflection.

The Letter of Application

If you are required to present a letter of application, be certain that it has a good layout or appearance and that its content is appropriate. A letter should be brief but not telegraphic, self-confident but not arrogant.

Layout/Appearance

A letter, like an essay or a resumé, provides a representation of you. It should look professional (i.e., neatly typed, having no mechanical errors in punctuation, spelling, or grammar). It should also have adequate white space and margins for easy readability. A visually attractive letter makes it more inviting for your reader to review its contents. Regarding its layout and length, follow these commonly approved practices:

- Your letter should be no longer than one page, single spaced. Because review committees are required to read scores of letters, they appreciate conciseness. Overlong letters may give the appearance that you are unsure of your eligibility and feel the need to "tell all"; in reverse, they may make you appear so self-confident that you have to give an endless inventory of your accomplishments.

- The standard format for a letter is three paragraphs or four at the most. Regarding length, the first and last paragraphs should be short, citing informational material such as why you are writing, where and when you can be reached, and so on. The second paragraph (the body) should provide more personal content. In this body paragraph you can project your individuality and mention achievements or interests that do not have a place in resumés or transcripts. (More detailed information on the content of paragraphs is given in the next section.)

The following are dos and don'ts about the overall content of your application letter:

- Do include essential information that is both specific and selective. Avoid using abstract phraseology that could apply to any applicant (e.g., "I am highly motivated, faithful, and hard working").
- Don't use inflated language (e.g., "Pursuant to your ad, I am initiating this application process herewith").
- Don't make demands (e.g., "It is imperative that you let me know of your decision by May 1").
- Don't sound arrogant (e.g., "You will surely be impressed by my credentials").
- Don't be obsequious (e.g., "I humbly request your kind consideration of my application").

Content

The recommended content for a letter is summarized here according to what each paragraph should contain.

First Paragraph

Begin your letter by stating exactly what you are applying for. If you request acceptance to a particular law school, internship, or other law-related appointment, mention a distinctive feature about it that interests you and for which you feel qualified (e.g., its areas of specialization, research, or legal aid programs). If possible, use legitimate name dropping (e.g., "Professor Johnson suggested that I contact you, since this internship will give me experience in historical research and cataloguing of bill initiatives").

Body Paragraph

When composing the body paragraph of your letter, consider the following points:

- Mention how your field of study and academic background qualify you as an applicant. Keep in mind the reviewer's perspective: The best way to judge how someone will perform in the future is to look at how he or she has performed in the past. Express an interest in having an interview so that you may learn more about the school (or firm or agency) as well as discover how you can best be a valuable participant, student, or researcher at that institution.

- Mention extracurricular activities that demonstrate related skills (e.g., writing skills, fluency in other languages, student government activities, sports leadership such as coaching or training, community volunteer work, etc.). These activities enhance your image as a well-rounded, civic-minded, and socially aware individual. If you have received awards or distinctions and they will appear on your resumé or transcript, do not feel you must enumerate them again in the letter.

- Mention the type of institution from which you have graduated or where you have studied. Attendance at schools, campuses, or institutes that are large and have diverse student bodies has prepared you for the world beyond academia, which is certainly diverse. This broad interactive experience will help you fit more readily into different types of work and study environments; therefore, cite this as an asset when you describe your educational experience.

Closing Paragraph

If it is relevant to your application, offer to submit samples of writing, reports, or other materials that further display your strengths. Finally, close your letter with a discreet request for an interview. Indicate your availability with regard to time, place, address, e-mail address, and phone number whereby you can be reached. When your letter is scanned, either by an individual or electronically, this kind of information is expected to be found at the end of your letter.

When you conform to these guidelines for a letter of application, you make it convenient for reviewers to locate items in suitable order. You have, consequently, introduced yourself in a communicative, reader-friendly manner.

EXAMPLE A.3 Student Letter

The following letter was written by a student applying for an internship under an administrative assistant to Congressman Philip S. Ireland. As you read it, determine whether it satisfies the preceding guidelines for writing a letter of application.

4206 Knott Rd. Apt. #4
College Park, MD 20740
November 11, 1997

Robert L. Howard,
Administrative Assistant
Office of Honorable Philip S. Ireland,
Member of Congress
1721 Longworth Building
Washington DC 20515

Dear Mr. Howard:

My name is Christopher Brownson and I am writing to express an interest in serving as an intern for Congressman Ireland this coming spring. Several long-time supporters of the Congressman have advised me that you are seeking interns for the spring session; I believe that my attached resumé demonstrates my eligibility for this opening.

My purposes in seeking this internship are quite simple. First, I am a lifelong resident of Congressman Ireland's district and would be honored to serve the people of northeast Pennsylvania. Second, I would like to gain experience in the field of government, and there is no better environment for gaining such experience than in the U.S. House of Representatives. I feel that I have much to offer Congressman Ireland, you, and your staff. As a Government and Politics major, I have had a number of courses in legislative procedure and history. Also, as my resumé indicates, I have had related work experience as an officer in the University of Maryland's Student Government Association. I would welcome the opportunity to meet with you to provide further details about my experience and to learn more about the agendas and research subject areas that you plan to assign to your spring interns.

Given brief notice, I am available for interview most afternoons and can be reached at (301) 555-1234. I look forward to hearing from you.

Sincerely,
Christopher J. Brownson
Christopher J. Brownson

Evaluation of Student Letter

This student letter meets the standards for a satisfactory letter of application. It is modest yet not unduly humble. It presents and locates the necessary information in an appropriate manner. In addition, it makes a good accompanying document for the resumé.

The Resumé

A good way to begin our discussion of guidelines for preparing an effective resumé is to read the following student sample and jot down what you consider are its strengths and weaknesses:

EXAMPLE A.4 **Student Resumé**

AVIATE M. PENA
3605 Wilkins Avenue
Arlington, VA 22207

<u>OBJECTIVE</u> To obtain a position consistent with my education, skills, and interests

<u>EDUCATION</u> It is my firm resolve to undertake graduate studies—most probably in attendance at law school
University of Maryland, College Park 9/95–present
Baccalaureate Degree anticipated 5/99
<u>Majors: English and Spanish</u>
Relevant classes include:

- Numerous Spanish language and literature courses
- English Critical Analysis
- Transitions to Democracy
- Speech Communication
- Women's History
- Legal Writing

	Paint Branch Senior High School, Arlington, VA <u>Honor Graduate (with Advanced Placement courses)</u> Extracurricular activities have included: assisting in organizing events for the Hispanic Student Union on campus; tutoring children who know no English; volunteer work with children at an orphanage; election to Review Board to disperse recreational funds to deserving campus groups; membership in the MaryPirg environmental society
<u>EMPLOYMENT</u>	During the years 1993-1998, I worked at a number of jobs in the summer as: nanny, hostess, office worker, party organizer, and receptionist, so as to assist in defraying educational costs. I estimate that I personally earned about 50 percent of my college expenses.
<u>SUMMARY/ PERSONAL</u>	I am hoping to be perceived as a hard-working, dedicated individual who is constantly eager for learning and acquiring new skills. In addition to the myriad of studies required in my dual majors, I have great interest in international law and environmental activities. Needless to state, I am utterly fluent—reading, writing, and speaking—in Spanish. Moreover, as my record bears evidence, I believe in community service, particularly as it applies to children. At this juncture of my life, I feel myself to be sufficiently able and well rounded so as to make a contribution to whatever organization engages my services.
<u>REFERENCES, ETC.</u>	Personal and business references, transcripts, and precise details of positions held are all available upon request.

Evaluation of Student Resumé

Although this resumé has a few good features, such as bullets of courses taken as well as highlighted and marginal headings, it does not successfully showcase this student, whose excellent background and skills deserve a better presentation. This resumé could be improved in the following ways:

- *Use of language:* The career objective statement placed at the beginning of this resumé needs to be more specific. Also, the overall writing in the resumé should contain more active verbs and less cliché-type verbiage. In addition, the passive voice should be eliminated (e.g., "I am hoping to be perceived as a hard-working, dedicated individual").
- *Sequencing of information:* The resumé needs a clearer ranking of order regarding the student's educational and work background. For example, it is not clear whether the listed extracurricular activities refer to the student's high school or college years. These activities would be better highlighted by bullets and itemized in chronological order.
- *The personal summary:* This student is fluent in Spanish, a qualification that enhances her potential in a variety of law-related fields. She should enumerate the professional areas where she can practice this capability.

The following student resumé makes a more positive impression:

EXAMPLE A.5 Student Resumé

ALICE LEE

Current Address:	Permanent Address:
3128 Queen Anne Hall	11125 Rosemary Lane
College Park, MD 20742	Gettysburg, PA 17325
(301) 555-4162	(301) 555-9580

Key Words: Bachelor of Science, Aerospace Engineering, Private Tutor, Treasurer, Instructor, Certificate for Child Development Clinician Training

Education: University of Maryland, College Park
B.S. Degree in Aerospace Engineering (expected May 1999)
Current Cumulative G.P.A. 4.0

Skills: Computer Languages: BASIC, FORTRAN, Mathematica
Computer Knowledge: WordPerfect 5.1, UNIX, Quattro Pro

Work Experience: **Private Tutor**
Instructed junior high and high school students in math lessons. Assisted college students with math/physics. (September 1994–1996)

Tutor
Harmony Cultural Institute, Inc. Gaithersburg, MD
Provided students with assistance and test-taking skills in after-school program. May 1993–June 1995)

Mentor
Montgomery County E.S.O.L. Public School Program
Tutored second-language-speaking students in English. (September 1993–June 1995)

Honors: Certificate of Academic Achievement (Phi Kappa Phi) (1996)
University of Maryland Honors Scholarship (Spring 1996)
Maryland Distinguished Scholar (1995)
Who's Who Among American College Students (1995)

Activities: Society of Women Engineers
Elected Officer: Co-Treasurer (September 1996–present)
Coordinate fund-raising activities, maintain accounts, compile resumé book, seek company sponsorship
American Institute of Aeronautics and Astronautics
Campus Crusade for Christ
Sigma Gamma Tau (Honorary Aerospace Engineer Society)

References: Available upon request.

Evaluation of Student Resumé

The format for this resume makes the important information both readable and visually pleasing. Here are some of the ways this is accomplished:

- The student's achievements are in bold print.
- Her work experience is described succinctly yet specifically.
- The use of partial sentences helps avoid personal pronouns (e.g., "Assisted college students with math/physics").

A Resumé Checklist

Resumé styles and formats are numerous. The kind you select should reflect your best qualities and qualifications; it should also be written to distinguish you from other applicants. Although you have much flexibility in developing a resumé, keep in mind these guidelines:

- Rank and sequence your information carefully, from most important to least important. Use reverse chronological order.
- Create an attractive resumé, using good bond paper, ample margins, and clearly distinguished headings or sections.
- Avoid ambiguous language. Use action verbs to describe your accomplishments, such as the following:

People	*Projects and Duties*
administered	established
conducted	wrote
promoted	coordinated
directed	modified
coordinated	analyzed
managed	investigated
adapted	monitored
collaborated	presided
programmed	initiated

- Use verbs that identify how you received a particular title or position (e.g., "*elected* president of the Student Government Association" or "*appointed* director of the Co-Op Center"). This establishes the source of your recognition (e.g., your *peers* elected you president or the *administration* appointed you director).

- Include the following in your contents:

Career Objective Statement	Activities
Education	Honors and Awards
Work Experience	Additional Skills

The Scannable Resumé

Before concluding this section on resumés, some mention should be made of electronic scanning. Computerized resumé searches are being increasingly used by law schools, organizations, and the corporate world at large. This means that computers rather than people will be the first to review your resumé. Scanners electronically select words and phrases from resumes to rank applicants; only those resumés that are singled out will be read by a person or committee. Therefore, it is a good idea to insert a Summary or Key Words section near the top of your resumé, in which the most important key words may be picked up electronically. (Perhaps you noticed that Alice Lee's resumé had a Key Words section.)

The Interview

Now that you have completed your essay, letter of application, and resumé, it is time to prepare for your interview(s). We will discuss the several stages of interviewing and how to prepare for each.

Preliminary Steps

Preparation and practice in interviewing will allow you to be more relaxed and confident during the actual interview. If there are orientation or interview workshops at your institution, plan to attend them. If not, you can prepare yourself with the following tips:

- Familiarize yourself with the law school, organization, or institution so that you can relate your strengths to the requirements of the position and ask the interviewer(s) well-thought-out questions.
- Review your own credentials so that you can answer questions about your background, experience, and strengths.
- Practice in front of a mirror or with friends or family what you will say in the interview situation.

Frequently Asked Questions

It is impossible to predict what sorts of questions you will be asked in an interview. However, the following list shows some of the questions commonly asked; you should be ready with prompt replies. Jot down ideas of some answers you might give if these questions were asked; doing so will help you avoid being momentarily stuck or returning a weak response in the actual interview:

1. Why are you interested in our particular law school (organization, internship, law firm)?
2. Why did you choose this field (major)?
3. What law-related courses did you like best? Least? Why?
4. Which of your skills or special abilities fit in with your career goals?
5. Have you held any leadership positions in legally related organizations?
6. What have you learned from some of the jobs you have held?
7. Tell us something about yourself.
8. What are your strengths? Weaknesses?
9. What have you done that best proves your initiative and willingness to work?
10. Describe a situation in which you had to use a particular attribute skillfully.
11. Why do you think we should accept you?
12. Describe what you think you will be doing career-wise 10 years from now.

Questions You *Should Ask*

During your interview, be positive and enthusiastic, especially if you are invited to ask questions. Do not retreat from this offer by saying "No, there isn't anything else I need to know. You have already answered any questions I might have had." It is preferable to demonstrate interest by making further inquiries; here are some suggested questions:

1. What would you say is the most important characteristic for performing well in this law school (internship, etc.)?
2. What opportunities will I have to practice my skills in real-life situations (e.g., community service programs)?
3. Will someone be paired with me during the first few weeks to assist me with questions I might have?

The Actual Interview

Keep in mind that first impressions are often lasting, or at least hard to change. Therefore, dress accordingly, project confidence in your voice and facial expressions, and smile! If possible, learn the interviewer's name in advance and address him or her by name when you meet and when you leave. Throughout the interview, maintain effective eye contact with your interviewer. Do not be afraid to make "small talk" or humorous observations in vacant spots of the interview, but always connect these little asides to the structure of the interview and your purpose for being there.

The Follow-Up Letter

It is a good idea to send a brief thank-you letter in which you reiterate your interest in the school (internship, position, etc.). This should be done within several days after the interview has taken place. In your letter, highlight your strengths and one or two things that stood out in the interview. Finally, conclude by indicating that you look forward to a response. However, if you are told by the interviewer, either in actual words or by innuendo, "Don't call us; we'll call you," comply with his or her wishes. In other words, if there is any indication that a follow-up letter might work against your favor, do not send one.

Taken together, the essay, the letter of application, the resumé, and the potential interview should introduce you to any reviewing committee as a desirable candidate. There is a great need in the legal field for students such as yourself to bring strong writing and research skills to the profession. Equally as important, there is a need for students such as yourself to write in a *language of justice*, not a *language of justification*.

EXERCISE

Evaluation of Student Application Essay

The following is a student essay submitted as part of an application to a law school; the school requested a personal statement by the student, giving his reason for applying. If you were on the admissions committee, how would you evaluate the essay?

Why I Am Applying to Law School

I never thought I would want to become a lawyer. This may have been because of brussels sprouts. As a child, I remember my Uncle Daniel, who graduated first in his class from law school, coming often to dinner, and my mother always serving his favorite vegetable: brussels sprouts. Talking for hours on end about trade policy and tariff negotiations, and boring me to tears, Uncle Daniel would fork sprout after hideous sprout into his mouth. Anything having to do with the law seemed dead, a bureaucratic rendition of a gigantic, beached brussels sprout.

Recently, however, a special opportunity came my way. I volunteered for an internship in a congressional office—mainly for the thrill of being on the Hill. My job was actually to sort and deliver mountains of mail. While delivering the mail, I had to wind my way through the maze-like tunnels of the United States Capitol. Everywhere I went, people were talking about one subject: the Law. Senators, Representatives, staffers, and lobbyists moved about as a sea of humanity through this labyrinth—all talking about the Law. When they discussed the Law, those visions of brussels sprouts began to vanish from my mind. These people knew more than the law; they knew how to *think*.

A few weeks after my internship had begun, I was given a task by one of the administrative assistants. A constituent had an inquiry about her mortgage, which had been transferred to an agency listed only as "The United States of America." Lack of payment, caused by the constituent's job loss when her textile plant closed, was the cause of this inquiry and her imminent "homelessness." It was my job to see if anything could be done to assist her. I had to call various banks and institutions, as well as consult volumes on Real Property law in her state. Suddenly, those identical-looking legal volumes became alive and interesting. I didn't understand everything I read, but I understood enough to consult a HUD reference. After talking to the original loan officer and to the county department of records, I was able to secure a note of temporary release for the constituent. I was elated that I was able to assist an ordinary citizen in a situation that arose from no fault of her own.

In the space of a few weeks, the Law had become transformed from a useless bureaucratic swamp into a living spring. I now want to be a part of this vibrant profession.

Evaluation of Student Essay

This essay conveys a sense of confidence and poise, indicating that the student is mature and prepared to confront challenges. His progress—from naively stereotyping an entire profession and its practitioners, to acquiring respect for that profession and its practitioners—is modestly and humorously related. Also, his narrative about the constituent's property problems represents a *concrete* example of how he "was able to assist an ordinary citizen."

Consider how much more genuinely committed this student seems than the student whose essay appeared earlier in this appendix (Example A.1: Application to West Virginia College of Law). In the former essay, the writer boasts that his "plans consist of making effective legal services available to all citizens regardless of their station in life." This self-congratulatory tone is not likely to persuade a review committee. Also, note that the author of Example A.1 wrote of what he will do in the *future,* whereas the author of the essay you just read gave an account of what he has *already done* to help a citizen in need.

APPENDIX B

Sample Papers

Throughout this book, when it seemed appropriate and useful, I inserted samples taken from assignments written by students in the Pre-Law Writing course at the University of Maryland. These samples served to demonstrate how certain principles or objectives, analyzed in the specific chapters, surfaced in the students' writing assignments. Some were illustrations of good models; others were illustrations of how various problems can be avoided in the legal writing process.

The purpose of this appendix is to provide examples of student papers that satisfied the main course assignments; as a group, they cover some of the most important features of legal prose. For the most part, they appear according to the order in which the strategies for writing legal prose are discussed in this text:

1. Legal definition
2. Thesis statement using legal definition for a position paper
3. Brief position paper
4. Long position paper

I believe they are fine examples of research, writing, and overall organization and I hope they will serve as useful guides for you in your own writing endeavors. (*Note:* Paragraph numbers in the left column are inserted for referral purposes in the evaluations that follow the samples.)

Legal Definition

The "Wetlands" Controversy

1 There are three types of wetlands that fit under the broad category of U.S. waters: *Non-Tidal wetlands, Private Tidal wetlands*, and *Tidal wetlands.*

1. *Non-Tidal wetlands* are inland areas inundated or saturated by excessive water. The continual flow of water in these non-tidal wetlands, provided by rain and underground water sources, allows the growth of a certain type of vegetation called *hydrophytic vegetation.* This vegetation form has specifically adapted to life in saturated soil conditions or *hydric soils.* These plants provide nutrients for fish and wildlife.
2. *Private Tidal wetlands* are areas that include land, not considered state or federal wetland, bordering on or lying beneath tidal waters. These lands are subject to tidal action and support aquatic growth.
3. *Tidal wetlands* are all state, federal, and private wetlands, marshes, aquatic vegetation, and lands affected by the rise and fall of tides from other water sources (Coggins, 1990, p. 15).

Wetlands and the Legal Controversy

2 There is an ongoing legal battle at the state and federal levels regarding laws that protect our wetlands. The battle focuses on the following questions: Does the government have a legal responsibility to preserve our fragile ecological system? Has the government overstepped its bounds concerning the rights of personal property owners and developers with regard to wetlands?

3 There is a conflict of interest between these two opposing forces as well as a difference of interpretation—by these two forces—of the environmental protection laws. Developers are charging what they designate as the "ill-defined attributes" of the laws to challenge the government's regulatory practices. But do their charges constitute a

firm legal basis for challenge? The following case, brought before the U.S. Court of Appeals in March 1997, is an example of the conflicting arguments surrounding this issue.

4 James J. Wilson, president of the $100,000,000 development company Interstate General, was charged with knowingly discharging fill material and excavated dirt (pollutants) into U.S. wetlands without a permit. He was found guilty of felony charges, fined $1,000,000, and sentenced to 21 months in prison and one year of supervised probation. Wilson appealed, claiming that these penalties were too strict; more importantly, he challenged the power of the U.S. District Court to regulate development according to the statute cited in his sentence. These were his points of contention: the questionable validity of the court's application of the Clean Water Act (Section 404) to wetlands not having a direct surface connection to other United States waters; and the validity of a ruling concerning a process known as "sidecasting," or the depositing of excavated material to wetland drainage ditches next to the ditches. Wilson, like other developers, argued that the phraseology and definitions of the wetlands laws are unclear and subject to scrutiny. Here, briefly, are the relevant provisions of these laws that were contested by Wilson.

5 First, an "individual" or "entity" (i.e., a developer) must obtain a permit from the federal government, in addition to meeting state and local requirements, before that developer can dump fill material into U.S. waters. By definition, wetlands fall into a special category regarding regulation of pollutants: "Unlike many other environmental laws that require a facility or project to attain a certain level of pollution control, wetlands determines whether the project itself will be allowed in the first place" (Dennison, 1990).

6 Second, the term "navigable waters," or "U.S. navigable waters," not only refers to coastal and main sources of water but to wetlands as well: "Federal regulation of wetlands has been called national zoning, not only because of its extensive coverage, but also because

of the criteria under which a permit application is reviewed" (Dennison, 1990, p. 435).

7 The two regulatory agencies that will jointly administer a wetland statute (known as Section 404, or the Clean Water Act) are the Army Corps of Engineers and the Environmental Protection Agency. Each of these agencies performs different tasks relating to wetlands usage. The Army Corps of Engineers reviews permit applications; this agency also carries out the majority of the enforcement responsibilities. The EPA develops standards for the issuance of permits but it also maintains the power to veto permit decisions made by the Army Corps of Engineers.

8 Developers argue that these two agencies have not yet successfully determined or agreed upon the exact ecological effects of development on wetlands areas. Moreover, they believe there is little similarity between wetlands and "U.S. navigable waters." For example, they challenge government rulings on what constitutes "saturated ground," since some wetlands do not visibly show surface water.

9 However, at this juncture, developers like James Wilson find that they have little or no legal footing on this issue. The reason for this can be attributed to the political interests of the opposing sides. The federal government is attempting to address the environmentalists' concerns and warnings; the developers are citing economic loss and sacrifice of jobs and revenue. Thus, despite the contestable language of the Clean Water Act, developers must continue to apply for permits and abide by the law as it stands until—or unless—definitional revisions expand the scope of the statute.

WORKS CITED

Coggins, George C. *Public Natural Resources Law* (New York: Clark Boardman Ltd., 1990).

Dennison, Mark S., ed. *1990 Zoning and Planning Law Handbook* (New York: Clark Boardman Ltd., 1990).

Evaluation of Legal Definition

(See Chapter 2 in this text, "Legal Definition.")

- Paragraph 1 provides a documented citation on the three types of wetlands as defined and described in *Public Natural Resources Law* (definition by legal authority).
- Paragraphs 2 and 3 expand the definition by stating the current points of conflict between the government and property owners who feel their rights have been violated (definition by issue).
- Paragraphs 4, 5, and 6 refer to a case in which a corporation president, questioning the validity of the Clean Water Act, discharged pollutants into a wetland and was given a court sentence. These paragraphs enumerate the provisions of the act that this president contested (definition by example).
- Paragraphs 7 and 8 explain that the Clean Water Act is administered by two agencies whose interpretations of the act are not entirely in agreement (interpretation of definitions).
- Paragraph 9 concludes by stating that unless or until revisions are made to the Clean Water Act, property owners have little or no ground for contesting charges made by regulatory agencies regarding their actions.

In its entirety, this definition of the wetlands controversy is developed through the use of several kinds of legal definition. However, the lead definition is *definition by legal authority,* on which the remaining definitions must hang. That is, any and all debates about wetlands must refer to the Clean Water Act.

Thesis Statement Using Legal Definition for a Position Paper

The following example shows how a student presented a thesis statement using legal definition to introduce his paper, which argues against the use of sterilization in the United States.

Thesis Statement on Sterilization

Definition of Sterilization

1 "Sterilization, the act or process by which one is rendered incapable of procreation, as for example, a vasectomy, touches upon the individual's right of privacy and the fundamental right to procreate, and has been characterized as being an extraordinary and highly intrusive form of medical treatment" (*56 Corpus Juris Secundum*, "Mental Health").

Thesis Statement

2 The "fundamental right to procreate" is inextricably bound to the fundamental right to life. To trespass upon the right to procreate, therefore, is to trespass upon the right to life. Thus, sterilization has been correctly characterized as "extraordinary and highly intrusive."

3 From 1934 to 1974, 62,000 Swedes were sterilized as part of a national program grounded in the science of racial biology and carried out by Swedish officials who believed they were helping to build a progressive, enlightened welfare state. This startling information has caused an international furor over the issue of state-sanctioned eugenics programs. However, forced sterilizations of the mentally ill are not restricted to countries outside the United States. In fact, the U.S. Supreme Court "has recognized a societal right to approve sterilization" (*C.J.S*, "Mental Health," p. 8).

4 There is even a compulsory sterilization statute in the United States which states that "The legislative authorization for the sterilization of mentally defective persons is a proper exercise of the police power, if constitutional requirements are met" ("Mental Health"). This statute derives from an opinion delivered by Justice Oliver Wendell Holmes, which sets out a series of requirements that any sterilization case must satisfy prior to the procedure (274 U.S., 200 *Buck v. Bell*). Justice Holmes's opinion is correct in that, if these requirements are carefully followed, an individual's Fourteenth Amendment right to due process has not been violated. But what the

opinion neglects to recognize is that the issue of sterilization goes beyond due process. It extends to the domain of "natural law."

5 This paper will argue that the right to procreate falls within the province of "natural law"—a higher law grounded in absolute moral rules—and that any law contrary to "natural law" is *not* law. To place this argument in historical context, I will first discuss "natural law" as it has been understood in the past two thousand years of western culture.

6 Following this background review, I will attempt to demonstrate how legal practice over the centuries has accommodated "natural law." Finally, I will address the current debates of controversies surrounding this subject, and specific cases in which government approval of sterilization still turns on the "natural law" issue.

WORKS CITED

Balz, Dan. "Sweden Sterilized Thousands of 'Useless' Citizens for Decades." *The Washington Post*, August 29, 1997, p. A1.

Evaluation of Thesis Statement

(See Chapter 5 in this text, "Writing the Argument.")

- Paragraph 1 introduces the legal definition of sterilization, taken from a legal encyclopedia.
- Paragraph 2 goes directly to the main point being made, stating outright that sterilization is a direct violation of the fundamental right to life.
- Paragraph 3 uses the example of a sterilization program in Sweden in which sterilization was performed on 62,000 mentally ill citizens over a 40-year period. The writer withholds his personal reaction to this, letting the statistics speak for themselves.
- Paragraph 4 briefly indicates what the U.S. legal and constitutional provisions are for sterilization. That is, the writer indicates how legal support for this procedure is problematized by questions of civic practicality versus personal liberty issues.

- Paragraph 5 concludes by arguing that sterilization is the desecration of a higher "natural law."
- Paragraph 6 is a transitional unit, linking the thesis statement to the main body of the paper, which will analyze the legal aspects of the sterilization debate.

Brief Position Paper

The following position paper deals with an issue that school boards around the nation are increasingly confronting: school prayer. For this writing assignment, students were asked to identify a *real* audience, making them aware that this was not just another "canned" exercise to be read by a faculty member. Instead, it was to be directed to an individual or group affected by the issue addressed in the paper. Indeed, the students were actually encouraged to forward their papers to the audiences they selected. This brought a greater vitality and sense of civic commitment to their projects.

To Pray or Not to Pray: School Prayer at Graduation

Audience: Chairman, Wotton High School Graduation Program Committee, Silver Spring, MD

Subject: Prayer in the June 1998 Graduation Ceremony

1 Although prayer has been known to play a traditional role in high school graduation ceremonies, it has come under considerable scrutiny in recent years. After decades of case law and Supreme Court interpretations of the Constitution, the courts have decided that organized prayer in public schools—including graduation ceremonies—shall not be permitted. The decision to prohibit prayer at graduation ceremonies is based on criteria set forth by the courts.

2 The essence of the debate over the legality of administering prayers at graduation ceremonies has its basis in the First Amendment of the Constitution, according to this passage:

> Congress shall make no law respecting an establishment of religion, or prohibiting the free exercise thereof.

Through vigorous analysis and interpretation of this part of the First Amendment, the courts have divided the portion addressing religion into two sections: the establishment clause and the free exercise clause (Schreck, 1995, p. 1869). These clauses seem to contradict one another; consequently, constitutional analysts have cast some doubts about the intentions embedded in the language of this passage.

3 The establishment clause is designed to provide a "wall of separation between church and state" (Ferdico, 1996, p. 12). The precedent used to decide whether any governmental or state controlled action violates the establishment clause was set forth by *Lemon v. Kurtzman* in 1971. Commonly referred to as the *Lemon* test, the criteria consist of three questions:

1. Is it the purpose of the governmental action to aid or promote religion?
2. Even if it is not the purpose of the action, is aid to or promotion of religion the primary effect of the governmental action?
3. Does the governmental action result in excessive entanglement with religion?

If the answer to *any* of these questions is yes, then the establishment clause has been violated. Here are some recent instances in which prayer at graduation ceremonies reactivated the debate surrounding these questions.

4 The legitimacy of voluntary prayer at graduation ceremonies was first put to the test in *Lee v. Weisman* in 1992. In this case, a middle school principal asked a rabbi to offer nonsectarian prayers at a *voluntary* graduation held on the school premises. This was understood to mean that students were not forced to attend their own graduation exercises. The Supreme Court determined that this case violated the establishment clause because state officials (in this case, school officials) directed performance of a formal religious exercise. Moreover, attendance and participation in the religious activity was in a real sense obligatory. The decision, rendered by Justice Kennedy, focused on coercion and divisiveness. Kennedy stated that the students were coerced into participating in the

ceremony because they had no other real alternative. He further ruled that choosing clergy from a particular sect had the potential for divisiveness. In a concurring opinion, Justice Blackmun added that the school's conduct violated the *Lemon* test, and that while government coercion is sufficient to prove violation of the establishment clause, it is not essential. That is, in this particular case, making attendance at the ceremony *voluntary* did not exonerate the school officials (Schreck, 1995, p. 1872).

5 In the wake of the *Lee* decision, many schools decided on another course of action: to have student-led prayer at graduation. As a way to avert the restrictions of the *Lee* decision, some schools turned the issue of graduation prayer over to the students: They themselves would both select and administer the prayers. Supporters of this practice thought this was a way to win the battle, insofar as it satisfied the free exercise clause of the First Amendment. But this only succeeded in generating further opposition to graduation prayers.

6 The first case involving student-led prayer was *Jones v. Clear Creek Independent School District*. In this case, the Fifth Circuit Court of Appeals ruled that high schools could deliver nonsectarian, nonproselytizing invocations at graduation ceremonies (Tanford, 1995, p. 447). The Fifth Circuit justified their decision by subjecting the facts of the case to the *Lemon* test. They found that the prayer had a secular purpose, did not advance religion, was not excessively entangled with religion, would not be perceived as government endorsement of religion, and that student-led prayer does not coerce participation.

7 However, the victory in *Jones v. Clear Creek* was short-lived. In *Gearon v. Loudoun County School Board*, the U.S. District Court for the Eastern District of Virginia decided the following: Although the students voted in favor of prayer, and the prayers were written and administered by students, that action was still unconstitutional. The Court reasoned that in spite of the students' entire management of the activity, authority had been granted by the state, thereby violating the establishment clause.

8 This brought another kink into the debate. With state-sponsored prayer banned, and student-led prayer considered to be government-endorsed coercion nonetheless, school boards began to allow students to decide by majority vote whether prayer should occur at graduation. This practice was tested in 1996 with *ACLU v. Black Horse Pike Regional School District.*

9 The Black Horse Pike Regional School District adopted a policy that allowed students to vote on whether a prayer should be included in the graduation ceremony. The students at Highland Regional High School voted in favor; they also decided on the content of the prayer. However, the ACLU joined a graduating senior to petition a federal court in New Jersey to block the prayer from the ceremony. The request was denied but the ACLU filed an emergency appeal, which was successful. The court entered a preliminary injunction prohibiting prayer at the graduation. The School Board appealed to the Third Circuit, but to no avail.

10 The court stated that although the state's involvement was less evident than in *Lee*, it did exist. Applying the *Lemon* test, the court rejected the school board's stated secular purpose of simply solemnizing the occasion. The court argued that there was no evidence to demonstrate that the occasion would be any less solemn without the prayer. In addition, the practice of a majority vote undermines the very intent of the establishment clause: to protect religious minorities (Schreck, 1995, p. 1873).

11 The preceding examples demonstrate how volatile the subject of graduation ceremony prayers has become. They also serve to emphasize the ambiguity that results when the First Amendment is broken down into the establishment clause and the free exercise clause. The courts—at a number of levels—have evaluated both sides of the equation and determined that the establishment clause takes precedence in the context of graduation ceremonies. In short, they have rejected state-sponsored prayer, student-led prayer, and student-led prayer based on majority vote. Therefore, it is both realistic and constitutional to ban public school prayer at graduation

ceremonies. As mentors to our graduates, we should demonstrate responsible, civic leadership and reject any efforts to violate such a strongly mandated policy.

WORKS CITED

Ferdico, John N. *Criminal Procedure for the Criminal Justice Professional* (New York: Garland, 1996).

Schreck, Myron. "Balancing the Right to Pray at Graduation and the Responsibility of Disestablishment." *Temple Law Review, 68* (1995): 1869–1892.

Tanford, Alexander J. "The Death of Graduation Prayer: The Parrot Sketch Redux." *Journal of Law and Education, 24.3* (1995): 424–454.

Evaluation of Brief Position Paper

This paper is addressed to a high school graduation program committee, arguing that the committee should reject any proposals to incorporate prayer in their future graduation ceremonies. The argument is basically laid out in two parts: (1) in a discussion and definition of the constitutional provisions relating to the issue of prayer in schools and (2) in a review of decisions on recent pivotal cases in which inclusion of prayer at graduation ceremonies was contested.

- Paragraph 1 states the courts' decisions in recent cases regarding prayer at graduation ceremonies. In a general summary, the paragraph claims that, for decades, the courts have rejected the idea.
- Paragraph 2 quotes a passage from the First Amendment that, because of its vague wording regarding the establishment clause and the free exercise clause, has been the source of controversy regarding school prayer.
- Paragraph 3 explains what criteria the *Lemon* test set forth in order to decide whether the establishment clause was being violated. This test acquired its name from a case in which three

questions were asked as a means of determining whether certain actions are a violation of the establishment clause.

- Paragraph 4 begins a section of the paper that summarizes recent cases in which school boards devised different methods for incorporating school prayer into graduation ceremonies.
- Paragraphs 5 and 6 discuss cases in which school boards tried to bypass First Amendment restrictions by allowing student-led prayer at graduation ceremonies.
- Paragraph 7 explains why student-led prayer was found to be unconstitutional in *Gearon v. Loudoun County School Board.*
- Paragraphs 8 and 9 discuss another strategy devised by school boards: to allow the *students* to decide by majority vote whether prayer should be included in graduation ceremonies.
- Paragraph 10 cites the specific reasons the Third Circuit Court rejected a school board's rationale for allowing school prayer at their graduation ceremony.
- Paragraph 11 concludes by demonstrating that the courts have consistently refused to find school prayer at graduation ceremonies to be constitutional, despite the different categorical arguments presented by school boards.

This paper, despite its brevity, manages to present the major legal points surrounding the issue in a clear, concise fashion.

Long Position Paper

The last student sample is a long position paper. Its strong advocacy pitch is directed at Nike, whose "Talk to Us" website—a comment exchange division—prompted the student to submit the project here proposed. The paper basically incorporates the components found in the preceding samples—definition, thesis statement, position paper, and related research—and synthesizes them into a persuasive document.

The student's outline for this paper is also included. Note that not all the headings and subheadings in the outline appear in the paper itself. Papers should deliver divisional headings for the reader's convenience; the number of headings used depends on the length and complexity of those divisions. Therefore, while a detailed outline helps *you*, the writer, organize the contents, only those headings that are necessary should be included for the reader to move easily from section to section of your paper. *Remember:* Writing an outline is an essential step in your prewriting stage (see Chapter 1).

Play Like a Girl:
Increasing Gender Equality in Sports

Purpose: To persuade Nike, Inc., to advocate full compliance from NCAA schools concerning Title IX and to propose a course of action for the company

Audience: Nike, Inc., "Talk To Us" Division, www.nike.com

I. Introduction
   A. Nike's accomplishments
   B. Need for more action
II. Title IX Definition
   A. Education Amendment of 1972, Title IX
   B. Civil rights guidelines
III. Results of Title IX
   A. Increased opportunities for women
   B. Increased participation by women
IV. Necessity of Nike's Support
   A. Violation of Title IX
   B. Challenges for school compliance
V. Proposal
   A. Expansion of "Play Like a Girl" Division
   B. Advertisement campaign
   C. Adopt a school
VI. Benefits for Nike
   A. Company image
   B. Increased market
VII. Conclusion

Dear Nike:

1 As a journalism major at the University of Maryland, a Nike customer, and a female athlete, I have noticed the various Nike advertisements promoting women's athletics. In both your TV advertisements and magazine ads, I have noted how you project strong images of women, playing hard. These images have inspired me.

2 Nike has made consistent steps toward gender equality in the sports arena with the "Play Like a Girl" website and "Girls Only" Sports Program. As a woman in love with sports and its benefits, I would like to suggest a plan of action that would intensify efforts to enforce Title IX and promote equality for women in sports.

Definition and Impact of Title IX

3 Popularly referred to as "Title IX," this segment of the Education Amendment of 1972 has drastically changed the nature of sports in schools. Section 901(a) of the law states, "No person in the United States shall on the basis of sex, be excluded from participation in, be denied the benefits of, or be subjected to discrimination under any educational program or activity receiving Federal financial assistance" (*U.S. Code*, 1972). The impact of Title IX has been unbelievable. The number of young women playing sports increased from 7 percent of total student athletes in 1972 to 35 percent by 1983. Participation more than quadrupled in just one decade (Miner, 1983). Also in 1972, the year Title IX was passed, no colleges or universities offered women athletic scholarships; just 10 years later, 15,000 scholarships were available from more than 800 schools (Miner, 1983).

4 The law was later interpreted by the Office for Civil Rights (OCR) and broken down into three areas of compliance. These three areas individually determine whether a collegiate athletic program is in compliance with Title IX; schools must be in compliance with all three areas to be eligible for federal funding.

5 The first area involves student participation in athletics. The number of spots in a school's athletic program for men and women

should be "substantially proportionate" to the number of men and women in the school's full-time, undergraduate student body (Shipley, 1997). Current interpretation has narrowed the term "substantially proportionate" to within a 5 percent comparative ratio (Lichtman, 1998). Under this first area, a school may be considered in compliance, even if it isn't "substantially proportionate," under either of the two following conditions. The school should either prove "a recent history of adding sports for the under-represented gender" or prove that it is "fully and effectively accommodating the interests and abilities of its students (Shipley, 1997).

6 The second area of the OCR's Title IX guidelines concerns scholarships. Simply put, the percentage of scholarship funds allocated to men and women should be substantially similar to the percentage of men and women in the varsity program (Shipley, 1997).

7 The third area, otherwise known as the "laundry list," demands equality in 11 other athletic program areas, including game and practice schedules, equipment and supplies, publicity, and coaching (Lichtman, 1998).

8 What is the purpose behind Title IX and women's equality in sports besides simple equality? In other words, why should girls and women play sports, beyond the fact that boys and men do? The intrinsic value of Title IX is that it provides women the choice to play sports, and to derive the consequential *benefits* from doing so.

9 The *1985 Miller Lite Report on Women in Sports* states that "women who are active in sports and recreational activities as girls feel greater confidence, self-esteem and pride in their physical and social selves than those who were sedentary as kids" (*Lifetime Online: Women's Sports Foundation*). Research has also suggested that female athletes experience less depression, are less likely to do drugs, and are less likely to have unwanted pregnancies. They are even more likely to graduate from high school and college than female nonathletes.

10 Yet, despite the many benefits female athletes have experienced from Title IX, many discrepancies in equality still exist. In February

1997, an eight-page questionnaire was mailed to National Collegiate Athletic Association (NCAA)-affiliated schools by the Women's Sports Foundation to evaluate the gender equality of each school in athletics. Of the 902 questionnaires sent out, 85 percent or 767 of the schools responded. The survey compilation was called the Gender Equity Report Card. The overall finding was that "many colleges and universities are allocating resources and opportunities at a roughly 2-1 ratio between male and female athletes despite the fact that women outnumber men on most campuses" (*Lifetime Online*).

11 While women made up 53 percent of all undergraduate students, they made up only 37 percent of all the NCAA athletes during 1995–96. During that same year, female athletes in this study received $142,622,803 less in scholarship aid than male athletes (this figure may also reflect the smaller representation of female athletes in the NCAA). And women's teams received only 26.6 percent of money spent on recruitment for all the NCAA divisions. Finally, in the area of coaching, about three-fourths of all the NCAA head and assistant coaches in the study were men; coaches of women's teams made $0.63 for every $1.00 earned by coaches of men's teams. Thus, it is estimated that 93 percent of colleges and universities are out of compliance in at least one the three areas of Title IX.

12 But the inequality is not only found in the athletic departments. It is also embedded in the media, which has long ignored women's sports and devotes less than *10 percent* of its coverage to women.

13 A frequent argument against Title IX is that equal opportunities for women means taking away from men's programs. This does not seem to be a valid argument. If a school cannot create more opportunities to balance out an uneven scale, then it must redistribute its resources.

14 But such arguments may be moot. The Gender Equity Report Card survey indicated that while more than 1,000 sports programs were added for women between 1978 and 1996, there was little change in men's programs. And, rather than blame women athletes

for any program cuts in men's sports, such cuts may be attributable to overspending in other areas of the men's sports operating budgets.

15 Another contention frequently raised against Title IX is that giving women a proportional amount of opportunity is ridiculous because "men have a greater interest in athletic participation than do women" (Marshall, 1997). Yet if this argument had been used in 1972 against Title IX, when a small number (7 percent) of high school women played sports, there might never have been a 28 percent increase in participation 11 years later. In the *Cohen v. Brown* majority opinion, Judge Hugh H. Bownes wrote, "As the athletes themselves have acknowledged time and time again . . . what stimulated this remarkable change in the quality of women's athletic competition was not a sudden, anomalous upsurge in women's interest in sports, but the enforcement of Title IX's mandate of gender equity in sports" (Cox, 1996).

Proposal for Nike

16 Like any other company, Nike seems to want a cutting-edge, pioneering attitude toward the field of sports. Women in sports *is* the next frontier. Nike should naturally want to play a leading role in this inevitable leveling of the "playing field" in the next century. Nike has the capability to contribute to this advancement for women in sports, not just act as a cheering bystander.

17 But, realistically speaking, what can Nike actually do? I suggest that Nike take an ambitious step toward promoting full compliance of Title IX in federally funded colleges and universities. "Title IX Project" is my proposal for such a step and contains three different programs involving three different publics. They are as follow:

18 1. The first program would be a national advertising campaign that ties the whole project together, exposing America to Title IX. Many Americans are unfamiliar with Title IX, especially its specific wording, and would need some basic information on the law and its

implications. Fortunately, Title IX's concise and straightforward language makes it easy to understand and to incorporate into advertisements or merchandise, like posters and T-shirts. By making Title IX more visible, Nike would equip society with some knowledge regarding a powerful piece of legislation. (In my personal experience, after reading the law and learning what Title IX stated, I found the words empowering.)

19 2. The second program would be an advertising campaign that informs college students of their school's compliance statistics. In ads placed in college newspapers, Nike could cite the provisions of Title IX and publish the particular college's figures for the following: the number of female students enrolled; the number of female athletes enrolled; and the scholarship dollars awarded to women athletes.

20 Although this would be a bold step, these ads would inform students about the state of athletic equality at their school. Not only would it heighten awareness concerning the issue but it would also work in a more specific, grass-roots manner, directed at a particular public. Moreover, the statistics (i.e., the "Gender Report Card") would give student activists a factual starting point to lobby for change at their institution.

21 3. The third program is the biggest and most complicated undertaking of the project. In an attempt to provide an example of change, to jump-start other schools into Title IX compliance, and to highlight how much needs to be done, Nike should *adopt* a school and help it comply with Title IX.

22 Nike would work with the school, brainstorming and developing an athletic program that would comply with Title IX after several years; this would involve developing a report that outlines the school's gradual compliance process. The study would eventually facilitate the compliance process at other schools by providing hindsight suggestions and methods for better progress at their schools. Here are some additional benefits that would result from Nike's project to adopt a school: (1) one more school would be in

compliance and would serve as a real-life example of efforts made, (2) other schools would be pressured to make compliance a priority, and (3) the project would provide the school, Title IX, and Nike with extended media coverage and positive exposure.

Benefits for Nike

23 There couldn't be a more perfect time for Nike to do something like this. Within the past few years, female athletes have made enormous strides at the Olympics: The United States sent more women to the Olympics than ever before, four female teams won gold medals, and, best of all, women's ice hockey had its debut in the winter 98 Olympics. It introduced a whole new sport for women and was a complete success with a gold medal victory.

24 Finally, the Women's National Basketball Association (WNBA) also took America by storm, doubling expected attendance at games during its 1997 summer debut. Therefore, women's sports have been scoring in more than one type of "court"; in at least four cases—the most recent being *Cohen v. Brown University* in 1996—the courts have favored the rights of female athletes and strict Title IX compliance. Although the "Title IX Project" would be an enormous undertaking for Nike, the organization has already been moving in that very direction in recent years. This project is just another way for Nike to showcase female athleticism.

25 Hanging in my room is a Nike poster of a woman running through the countryside; on it are these words: "There are clubs you can't belong to/ Neighborhoods you can't live in/ Schools you can't get into/ But the roads are always open./ Just do it." Nike, we women say to you: "Just do it." Help to keep the roads open for female athletes and to pave new ones for the future.

WORKS CITED

Cox, Gail. "Brown U. Ruling Preserves Big Mo in Female Sports." *National Law Journal, 19.5* (1996): 1627–1644.

"Education Amendments of 1972, Title IX." *United States Code: Congressional and Administrative News, 92nd Congress, Second Session 1972* (St. Paul: West Publishing, 1972).

Lichtman, Brenda. "Sexual Discrimination and School Sports: The Title IX Compliance Challenge." *USA Today Magazine*, March 1998, p. 62.

Marshall, Alison B. "Title IX and Gender Discrimination in Athletics." *Employee Relations Law Journal, 23.1* (1997): 93–103.

Miner, Barbara. "Supreme Court to Rule on Women's Sports Aid." *United Press International*, December 27, 1983, Sports Section.

Shipley, Amy. "Playing Field Levels at Texas." *The Washington Post*, July 6, 1997, Section A.

Evaluation of Long Position Paper

This student shows bold initiative: Given her youthful status as a college undergraduate, she nonetheless has the confidence to present an original and ambitious proposal to one of the nation's largest corporations. Here are the strategies she employed to argue her points effectively:

- Paragraphs 1 and 2 project a convincing ethos (voice) of the author, emphasizing how Nike's promotional efforts toward women athletes have inspired her. She then expresses the belief that because of Nike's encouraging invitation to interact on "Play Like a Girl," Nike would be willing to listen to her proposal.
- Paragraphs 3–7 present the student's support for the proposal (a legal document): the segment of the Education Amendment of 1972 known as Title IX. Consequently, she brings direct quotations from this law, which specifically indicate how colleges and universities must comply with gender allotments and entitlement in sports.
- Paragraphs 8 and 9 are the transitional section of the paper. The writer refers to the psychological and sociocultural advantages for women when they participate in sports.

- Paragraphs 10–12 present the author's proof that despite the law, most colleges and universities are still out of compliance. Note that her proof is substantiated by *legal* requirements that promote the cause of female athletes as well as the *positive effects* derived from participating in sports.
- Paragraphs 13 and 14 reply to and refute counterarguments regarding Title IX.
- Paragraph 15 gives added weight to the author's appeal by quoting from a (favorable to women) court decision pertaining to Title IX regarding a university's neglect of female athletes.
- Paragraphs 16–22 explain the specifics of the author's proposal. This is the most important section of the essay; in order to prove effective, it must be cogent and realistic in its suggestions.
- Paragraphs 23–25 close the essay with a direct plea to Nike, emphasizing how not women athletes alone, but the Nike Corporation itself, will benefit from this proposal.

Glossary of Legal Terms

The following is a selective list of legal terms that appear in this text and require clarification. They are mainly technical terms whose meanings in legal parlance are different from their meanings in everyday usage. This list is not exhaustive and should be supplemented by a standard legal dictionary.

Actionable Refers to wrongful conduct that may form the basis of a proceeding or lawsuit; gives rise to a cause of action.

Authority The express or implied permission or power delegated to another (e.g., a power of attorney document); also refers to the jurisdictional authority of a particular court.

Case law The law as set forth in cases that have been decided. Case law is based on judicial precedent rather than on statutory laws, which are legislative in origin.

Code A systematic collection or revision of laws, rules, or regulations, classified according to their subject matter (e.g., the motor vehicle code).

Curtilage The land around a house or dwelling protected by the Fourth Amendment of the Constitution against searches and seizures.

Dictum A statement, remark, or observation in a judicial opinion that is neither necessary to the case nor binding in subsequent cases.

Facts Events or circumstances whose actuality or happening must be determined and verified by evidence (e.g., the testimony of witnesses).

Holding The result reached by a court in resolving a case before it; sometimes used interchangeably with *decision,* which refers to results in a more general sense.

Issue A single, certain point of fact that is disputed between parties to the litigation.

Jurisdiction The power to hear and determine a case. There are different types of jurisdictions (e.g., territorial jurisdiction or the territory over which a government may exercise power or control). The term is commonly used in two forms: to refer to a court system and to refer to the power of a court or court system to adjudicate.

Legislative history The compilation of recorded events that lead to the passage of a bill; helps analysts determine the origin and meaning of a particular statute.

Opinion The reason given for the court's decision; usually implies that it was agreed upon by the majority of the judges (e.g., a concurring opinion).

Pleadings Statements, in legal format, of the plaintiff's cause of action as well as of the defendant's ground of defense.

Precedent The basis for the system of jurisprudence in the United States; a formerly decided case that is recognized or relied on as authority in future cases that present the same legal problems.

Presumptive evidence Evidence that is not conclusive; may require further evidence to establish its truth and sufficiency.

Privilege An exemption or immunity from some form of legal compulsion; protects communication confidentiality (e.g., executive privilege and attorney/client privilege).

Statute An act of the legislature, which, by prescribed means and in conformity with constitutional authority, is intended to promote the general welfare.

Stay A judicial order in which an action is forbidden or held in abeyance until some future determination.

Terms of art Words in the law that have particular meanings to particular areas of the law (e.g., preemptive rights and prayer for relief).

Tort A private or civil wrong or injury for which a civil action is a remedy. Elements by which torts are classified include intent, negligence, and liability.

Index